KU-624-203

Privileging Difference

Antony Easthope

Edited by Catherine Belsey

palgrave

© Diane Easthope and Catherine Belsey 2002

All rights reserved. No reproduction, copy or transmission of
this publication may be made without written permission.

No paragraph of this publication may be reproduced, copied or
transmitted save with written permission or in accordance with
the provisions of the Copyright, Designs and Patents Act 1988,
or under the terms of any licence permitting limited copying
issued by the Copyright Licensing Agency, 90 Tottenham Court
Road, London W1T 4LP.

Any person who does any unauthorised act in relation to this
publication may be liable to criminal prosecution and civil
claims for damages.

The author has asserted his right to be identified
as the author of this work in accordance with the
Copyright, Designs and Patents Act 1988.

First published 2002 by
PALGRAVE
Houndmills, Basingstoke, Hampshire RG21 6XS and
175 Fifth Avenue, New York, N.Y. 10010
Companies and representatives throughout the world

PALGRAVE is the new global academic imprint of
St. Martin's Press LLC Scholarly and Reference Division and
Palgrave Publishers Ltd (formerly Macmillan Press Ltd).

ISBN 0–333–78628–9 hardback
ISBN 0–333–78629–7 paperback

This book is printed on paper suitable for recycling and
made from fully managed and sustained forest sources.

A catalogue record for this book is available
from the British Library.

Library of Congress Cataloging-in-Publication Data
Easthope, Antony.
    Privileging difference/Antony Easthope; edited by Catherine Belsey.
       p. cm.
    Includes bibliographical references (p.) and index.
    Contents: Duchamp—Heath—From Marxism to difference—Said—
Bhabha—Rose—Haraway—Braidotti—Butler—Dollimore—Eagleton—
Grossberg—Zizek—The two Jakes [Lacan and Derrida].
    ISBN 0-333-78628-9 — ISBN 0-333-78629-7 (pbk.)
       1. Deconstruction. 2. Poststructuralism. I. Belsey Catherine. II. Title.

PN98.D43 E19 2001
149—dc21   2001036985

10 9 8 7 6 5 4 3 2 1
11 10 09 08 07 06 05 04 03 02

Learning Resources
Centre
1223577 b

Printed in China

Contents

Acknowledgements

Thanks go to Gary Banham, Stuart Crehan and Kate McGowan for reading and criticising sections. It's difficult to measure my debt to Catherine Belsey for innumerable chats about these matters. Nor the immense gratitude I felt when the real came to claim me back again (as does happen) and she agreed to tidy up what she could and see the book through the press.

ANTONY EASTHOPE

The editor and publishers wish to thank the following for permission to use copyright material:

Faber and Faber, for the extract from 'Daddy' from *Collected Poems* by Sylvia Plath. Reproduced by permission of Faber and Faber Ltd. HarperCollins Publishers, for the extract from 'Daddy' from *Ariel* by Sylvia Plath, copyright © Ted Hughes, 1963. Reproduced by permission of HarperCollins Publishers, Inc.

Every effort has been made to trace the copyright holders but if any have been inadvertently overlooked the publishers will be pleased to make the necessary arrangement at the first opportunity.

Foreword

On Thursday, 9 December 1999, we were waiting for the doctor to arrive to see Antony. We were also racing to finish *Privileging Difference*. I was trying to get a handwritten chapter of the book onto the computer and checking individual words with Antony from time to time. Our daughter Kate was transcribing a series of changes to the final chapter at his dictation.

The doctor arrived just as we were finishing at midnight. He made it clear that Antony could only be made more comfortable in hospital, but Antony did not want to go. The book was finished, but he still wanted to discuss details of the editing with Kate Belsey, who was due to travel up to see him the next day. His father, who was eighty-seven, was also expected to arrive by plane the next morning. However, I had to call the doctor back at four in the morning and this time Antony agreed to go into hospital.

Antony's decline from then on was rapid. He refused a stronger pain-killer drip so that his head would be clear enough for his discussion with Kate Belsey on Saturday, but after that his only concern was to go home to die. We were able to get him home on Monday evening, and he died the following morning.

Privileging Difference was extremely important to him. He wrote much of it while he was ill, sometimes sitting at the computer for short periods to type, later writing in longhand, leaning on his elbow to do so and then dictating onto tapes.

Antony was deeply committed to the case it makes. He would have been very glad to see it in print.

DIANE EASTHOPE

Editor's Preface

Why doesn't a radical work remain radical? How is it that the edge of experimentalism is so easily blunted? Why do we constantly need a new avant-garde, as the old becomes aestheticised, recuperated?

The answer is that the subject is always impelled towards recovery of the mastery threatened by the opening of a gap in its seamless apprehension of the world. We 'make sense' of what was once so shocking. The Lacanian imaginary, jubilant in misrecognition, affirms that all is well, that the fixed and restricted point of view from which we look is truly omniscient and that what we see is all there is. The imaginary, triumphantly seizing hold of thematic meaning, occludes the challenge to our apprehension posed by radical form.

Something similar happens to new theories. Difficult, scandalous or impenetrable at first, they are rapidly either assimilated or superseded. Too rapidly, Antony Easthope argues. The constant impulse of theory, like modernist art, to make it new, the desire for each radical intervention to surpass the last, means that we all too easily leave behind insights that have not exhausted their capabilities. The poststructuralist insistence on difference, rigorous in its initial impulse, turned into an opportunity to do theory the easy way, securing credibility by embracing variety, while bypassing the radical questions poststructuralism initially raised. Easthope's argument is that an imaginary version of deconstruction, privileging difference, has led to a celebration of the option of endless diversity, without regard for the binary oppositions such work itself fails to deconstruct. The privilege so easily accorded to heterogeneity depends on a silent and undeconstructed antithesis between sameness (bad) and difference (good), between dominance (evil) and subversion (virtuous), and between metaphysics and deconstruction itself.

The effect is utopian, in both senses of that term: optimistic in its commitment to radical change; hopeless, in its failure to engage with the problems concerning textuality itself that have been so carefully worked though in the light of psychoanalytic theory. Before we can make an adequate analysis of the present, or seriously consider the possibilities for the future, we need, Easthope affirms, to reckon with three terms that are too easily ignored: the signifier, the imaginary and the subject.

Recent theories and practices of interpretation readily revert, he argues, to an account of thematic content, neglecting the text's mode of address and the position it thereby offers the reader-subject. Going straight to the signified, confined to what the text *says*, such reading is unable to recognise what the text *does*, its forms of reassurance, or the surprising role of the signifier in resisting the imaginary mastery which so soon reappears to insulate the subject against the effects of shock.

The rapid assimilation of poststructuralist theory has proved disappointing in two main ways. On the one hand, a residual humanism ignores the textuality of the text, which is then reread as delivering another 'truth' that confirms the mastery of the reader-subject. On the other, a celebration of difference for its own sake has, ironically, much the same effect. Here the interpretation produced puts on display the ingenuity of the interpreter, at the expense of the text's capacity to disturb. Both tendencies ignore the difficult task of reading itself, the role of the reader's desire in the process, and the opportunities offered by Lacanian psychoanalysis for understanding texts as complex performatives, now promising, now withholding, the mastery we long for.

The book concludes with a contrast between what Easthope calls the two Jakes, Jacques Lacan and Jacques Derrida, the one anarchic, unpredictable, radically disrupting his own moment, the other an attentive reader, scrupulous, brilliantly engaged with the important issues of his society, as well as the history of philosophy. But this is not only a contrast. Easthope analyses what is also an important relationship and, paradoxically, given what we know of their personal exchanges, one which need not immediately divide our allegiances. What, he asks, is the connection between Lacan's big Other, the order of language and culture, constitutive for us but empty of substance, and Derrida's differance (with an 'a'), relegating meaning beyond reach? If we need Derrida for the precision with which he desires and distrusts presence, we need Lacan's account of the subject which seeks and discounts imaginary mastery.

Revising the typescript for publication has been in many ways a real exercise in nostalgia for me. Antony Easthope's tones are clearly audible in the book, and issues we discussed surface again and again. Tracking down the references, too, was like delving into my own past. *Screen* in the 1970s, the first issue of the short-lived *Ideology and Consciousness*, and *For Marx* from 1969 were all on my shelves, their spines often broken and their pages brown with age. It was good to reopen them and reflect on how much has changed for the better since the days when it seemed inconceivable that things would ever alter in the academy.

But this is a book about the present, not the past. One after another, it takes issue with authors who have come to prominence by ignoring, Easthope argues, the relation between the text and the reader, and the complexity of subjectivity itself. To privilege difference, without attention to what it is that difference enacts, is to make our work, he claims, too often facile.

The book pulls no punches. Easthope knew that it was his own last chance to intervene in the way we not only 'do' theory but also interpret our culture. With conviction, and entirely without malice, he offers close textual analyses of the major theorists of our time, acknowledging their importance, but stressing their blindnesses too.

His instructions to me concerning the preparation of the book for publication were characteristically direct, clear and non-negotiable. I was to check the typescript for grammar, typos, errors, *non sequiturs*, and no more. I have therefore not attempted to impersonate him, ventriloquise, modify, censor or change the argument in any way. The opinions which follow are his.

Sometimes they coincide with mine. And sometimes they don't. But in all instances, I have found them sharp, vigorous and challenging. They have frequently made me rethink my own views. And I have enjoyed the directness, the clarity and the wit of the writing.

The main problem was hunting out the references. The authors and dates were all there in the text, but they rarely coincided with anything in the bibliography. I gratefully acknowledge the people who have helped me track down or confirm the wit and wisdom of a range of writers, especially Neil Badmington, Claire Connolly, Nicholas Daly, Laurent Milesi and Simina Milesi, and those authors who have responded to my e-mails asking them where they said what. Diane Easthope, who succeeded in making sense of Antony's handwriting and the tapes of his revisions, has been a tower of strength in this, as always.

The dedication of the book is Antony's. But if I am permitted to dedicate my own small part in its preparation, it would be to John, Mike and Rob, the other comrades.

I am definitely allowed to add an account of the reasons why my intervention has been necessary at all. Antony's death on 14 December 1999 left the references unchecked and the body of the text unrevised. Here again his instructions were decisive: 'Explain only – asking for no special favours except to let the argument be judged on its merits.'

And he added laconically, 'In doubt, try a séance.' I have managed without. But in the event that readers seek further enlightenment on any aspect of what follows, they may choose to take up his offer.

Catherine Belsey

1 Duchamp

At the beginning of the year 1920, I arrived back in Paris, extremely glad to see my friends again. . . . The début of Dadaism in Paris took place on the twenty-third of January, at the matinée organised by the Dadaist review *Littérature* . . . . Picabia, who has undergone so many influences, particularly those of the clear and powerful mind of Marcel Duchamp, exhibited a number of pictures, one of which was a drawing done in chalk on a blackboard and erased on the stage .

So Tristan Tzara in 1920 in his 'Memoirs' (1992: 233). By that year the clear and powerful mind of Marcel Duchamp had already made its presence felt with a bicycle wheel inverted and mounted on an ordinary four-legged wooden stool (*Bicycle Wheel*, 1913), and (now almost too well known to require description) the bell-shaped, shiny, white porcelain men's urinal, submitted for exhibition in New York in 1917 under the title *Fountain* and signed 'R. Mutt'. This lies on a horizontal plane and not attached vertically to the wall, as it would be if it were to be plumbed in and used; the original got destroyed but copies can be seen in the Musée Maillol in Paris, and elsewhere.

Duchamp's readymades offered the most powerful affront to the traditional art of museums and galleries. Devoid of interiority, the readymade is manufactured, impersonal, openly subject to contingency. While Duchamp's *The Large Glass* (begun in 1915, and 'finally unfinished' eight years later) was being taken back to its owner after exhibition in 1926, it was damaged, leaving a network of fine lines across the figurations: welcoming this intervention from chance, Duchamp proclaimed that his work was now 'completed' (Judovitz 1995: 52).

In the West in the early years of this century traditional art was committed to a serious ideal of beauty raised above the ordinary world, to individuality, the expression of personality and the private self. To presence. Illusionist and elitist, such art solicited its viewer into the pleasures of passive consumption. Dada, in contrast, powered by Duchamp's iconoclastic vision, was anti-illusionist, democratic, social, insisting on itself as produced by labour, stressing the body, open to the comic, trying to compel an active response from those who encountered it. According to Tzara, at the Dada Festival at the Salle Gaveau in 1920 the audience threw not only eggs but also beef-steaks: a photograph taken shows 'everybody in the house waving their arms and with their mouths open shouting' (1992: 236).

The Dada manifesto issued in Berlin in 1918 asserted that 'Dadaism for the first time has ceased to take an aesthetic attitude toward life' (cited Richter 1965: 106). Duchamp describes his readymades as 'based on a reaction of *visual indifference . . .* a complete anaesthesia' (the word alluding to the absence of the aesthetic) (cited 89). Hans Richter says:

> With Picabia the words 'Art is dead' seem always to be followed by a faint echo: 'Long Live Art'. With Duchamp the echo is silent.   (91)

It was Duchamp, after all, who coined for Dadaism its most savagely anti-art slogan: 'use a Rembrandt as an ironing board!' (cited 89).

But getting rid of Rembrandt is not that simple. Richter sounds a warning when he recalls that, if anyone did try 'to extract aesthetic pleasure . . . from these readymades', Duchamp's reaction was: 'Let him!' (cited 88). It is Richter again who points out that since 1917 the *Fountain* 'has been the centre-piece of countless exhibitions', and that

> at the Dada exhibition . . . in the late 'fifties, it hung over the main entrance. . . . No trace of the initial shock remained.   (89)

After a New York exhibition in the early 1960s, which included Andy Warhol and Claes Oldenburg, Duchamp wrote to Richter in a letter of 10 November 1962:

> When I discovered readymades I thought to discourage aesthetics. . . . I threw the bottle-rack and the urinal into their faces as a challenge and now they admire them for their aesthetic beauty.   (cited 207–8)

He was right. The works of Duchamp are shown in galleries and exhibitions throughout the world; if lost or damaged, they are lovingly retouched and restored. Just like a Rembrandt.

What went wrong? Is there something here that will always go wrong?

Completing the seemingly incomplete

A men's urinal in a lavatory is simultaneously a physical object for use and a sign. But a men's urinal disconnected from water pipes and outlet, laid on its side and inserted into an art gallery, is a physical object to be used mainly as a sign. In order to draw a line between sign and physical object, we do not need an absolute distinction or some foundation in a binary opposition. Until there is telepathy, it will not be possible to communicate signs without physical means (sound waves in the case of speech); in fact, even with telepathy, there would have to be at least something physical in the form of signifiers shared and so capable of being transmitted from one head to another (just as there cannot be unspoken internal consciousness without signifiers).

Such physicality means that what may be primarily intended as a sign can be employed for its physical properties. Cromwell's soldiers used old St Paul's Cathedral to stable their horses; famously, some of Marx's manuscripts held in Berlin were made part of the barricades in the Spartacist rising. But a Rembrandt would quickly turn into a very sticky and unsuccessful ironing board. And you weren't invited to pee in Duchamp's *Fountain*.

In 1993 Pierre Pinoncelli did exactly that. At the opening of a new art gallery in Nîmes, Pinoncelli walked up to Duchamp's *Fountain*, urinated in it, and hit the porcelain several times with a hammer. He claimed he attacked the work to liberate it, not to destroy it. His act, he declared, was 'an iconoclastic gesture in the spirit of Duchamp, the living Duchamp, not the one who is adored, embalmed in museums like a desiccated royal mummy, the Tutankhamun of modern art' (*Guardian*, 6 March 1999).

Pinoncelli's physical action was also symbolic. Similarly, Duchamp's material thing mainly constitutes an act of signification, a text. As such, it aims to open a gap between two contexts of meaning. One is to do with galleries, art and beauty; at the same time, another asks for it to be read in relation to the body and excretion, to the intimate familiarity of the private world of the men's urinal, the male bond, phallic exchange ('How high up the wall can you . . . ?') and all that Freud has to say about men and urination. The *Fountain* marks a disjunction, effecting a possible place of difference and alterity.

The theme of my general argument can be stated briefly: it is not possible for human beings, for speaking subjects, to encounter such a gap in signification without immediately trying to close it with fantasy, to recuperate it into some form of coherent meaning. And I would propose that any view which does not take adequate account of this effect can be accused of privileging difference.

Every human culture has worked up a specialised rhetorical strategy for naming the seemingly unnameable and denying alterity. We inherit a handbook of terms constructing the other as supernatural, numinous, taboo, magic, spirit (good or evil). Modernity has fostered a more secular vocabulary of commination: 'horror', 'disgust', 'bestial', 'amazing', 'shocking', 'uncanny'. If none of these will stick, there is always 'inhuman'. I like Tristan Tzara's exaggerated description of the Dada Festival in 1920, when people threw things, waved their arms and shouted. Expressions of shock or denial or attempted expulsion are a basic, if clumsy, manoeuvre for maintaining an imaginary which seems threatened. Familiarisation, recognition, assimilation into the same, naturalisation are perhaps more widespread moves, and that is precisely what Richter and Duchamp are forced to admit has happened to the *Fountain* between 1917 and the 1950s: 'No trace of the initial shock remained', 'I threw the bottle rack and the urinal into their faces as a challenge and now they admire them for their aesthetic beauty'. Human beings cannot bear too much reality (or not, as I shall argue later, without risking trauma).

This inescapable endeavour to fill in any suggestion of a crack in signification is a function of what Jacques Lacan terms 'the imaginary'. Even at the risk of rehearsing what is already well known, I need to recall a clear outline of what is implied in this conceptualisation.

The imaginary

Each term in Lacan's teaching is more like an English April than a concept: every year it's different. A useful approach to his notion of the imaginary is through the marriage he attempts to solemnise of Saussurian linguistics with the subject's split between conscious and unconscious.

Saussure distinguished between the level of the shaped *sound* of a word (the signifier) and the *meaning* attached to it (the signified); together signifier and signified form a completed sign. When talking, we can't think about the signifiers we're using: we just 'express' ourselves. In Lacan's account, once we enter language, our needs always have to 'pass through the defiles of the signifier' (1977a: 264). Hence his specification of the signifier:

> the definition of a signifier is that it represents a subject not for another subject but for another signifier. This is the only definition possible of the signifier as different from the sign. The sign is something that represents something for somebody, but the signifier is something that represents a subject for another signifier.
>
> (1972: 194).

Signifiers are based in phonemes and, according to Saussure, 'are characterised . . . by the fact that they are distinct'; they are 'opposing, relative, and negative entities' (Saussure 1992: 12). Phonemes and signifiers relate in the first place to each other in an autonomous system which has no interest in meaning. The sign, representing 'something for somebody', does occur but is a secondary effect. Lacan would identify the completed sign as the place of consciousness and the signifier as the place where the unconscious operates, making conscious meaning possible by being excluded from it. The split conscious/unconscious is like the bar which separates signifier and signified, where big S is the signifier and little s the signified underneath it:

$$\frac{S}{s} \quad \text{(1977a: 149)}$$

The subject appears present to itself in the signified and completed sign, but is lacking or barred from itself in the signifiers and their differences; here 'it speaks', for the unconscious is 'a play of the signifier' that appears in 'dreams, slips of tongue or pen, witticisms or symptoms' (Lacan 1977b: 130).

Lacan also asks us to think the bar or split between conscious and unconscious in relation to the linguistic distinction between enunciation and enounced – *'énonciation'*, the process of utterance, and *'énoncé'*, what is stated in the content of the utterance (see Easthope 1983: 40–7). Two positions for the speaking subject should be distinguished, one as subject of the signifier, or process of enunciation, another as subject of the signified, or enounced, or statement. Someone who says 'I am lying' is not committing themselves to paradox for, as Lacan points out, 'the *I* of the enunciation is not same as the *I* of the statement' (*énoncé*) (1977b: 139), though the two positions for the *I* happen to be designated by the same shifter, the first person pronoun. Another example, perhaps, would be 'I am joking'. One implication of the use of the terms is that the subject as represented in the statement is always sliding away from the subject produced in the act of representing itself. Another is that what a text thinks it is stating may tell a very different story from what is otherwise said in its own rhetoric.

Lacan's term 'imaginary' specifies the huge and inescapable mode of fantasy in which the subject finds meaning apparently present to consciousness; and 'symbolic' defines the organisation of signifiers which makes this possible and of which it is an effect. The imaginary is the domain in which the ego seems to be the same in space, permanent across time, and unified in substance, thus misrecognising itself as a full identity, imagining it speaks directly. The symbolic is the domain of culture, all the rules and meanings which exist 'out there' before I arrive, a particular structure of signifiers, the Other. The gaps and differences between the signifiers in language introduce lack into the speaking subject, a form of absence it must try to make good as imaginary presence. The alternative is psychosis or death.

Though in a sense everyone lives out their own imaginary dispositions, subjects take part in a shared identification, so that the Lacanian imaginary is also a comprehensive and collective effect. It would be an exaggeration to say that what we take to be reality is an illusion, though the reality our lived and experienced perception returns to us is permeated by fantasy elements and supported by the signifiers of the symbolic system. It is temptingly easy, especially in Western culture, to think of reality as consisting of discrete entities 'out there'. But the perception of the world in this way is enormously helped by our species capacity to single out apparently fixed objects and acknowledge their presence according to the signs conventionally used for them ('cat', 'critic', 'hearth-rug'). Maurice Merleau-Ponty shows that the other animals can't do this because what is 'lacking in the animal is the symbolic behaviour which it would have to possess in order to find an invariant in the external object' (1965: 118). The existence for us of such seemingly self-defining objects excludes the effect of time and space. Restore that, and objects are always in a state of becoming.

Modern Western common sense organises time into a linear chronology of hours, days, years, within a structure of shared fantasy. This is held in place by the movement of the sun, together with a mythical but altogether effective anchoring point, the year of the birth of Jesus (other cultures manage just as efficiently with a different regulatory date-line). On this basis, whether we want to or not, we get up for work, watch television programmes and take Saturdays off. If you believe in it, it works.

So also with classic Newtonian space. Inches, yards and miles (will these be superseded by centimetres and kilometres?) allow latitude to be mapped between anchoring points in the North and South poles, just as longitude is pinned to the Greenwich meridian (for a reason no less arbitrary than that the Brits got there first).

We could hardly move today without this imaginary calibration. The anchoring points designating time and space have almost inescapable authority, which the individual subject has little choice but to submit to. But because it is upheld only by the system of signifiers, reinscription is always feasible. In more obviously social terms, other anchoring points define class, gender, ethnicity, nation, family and so on, though these are not so apparently universal as those for space and time. (I would anticipate an important intervention along the lines of development from Lacan proposed by Ernesto Laclau and Chantal Mouffe (1985), trying to map the shifting relations of anchoring points in the social formation.)

None of this changes the basic process by which a signifier represents a subject for another signifier. The imaginary is not an object out there in the world, nor simply an effect of the subject, but both together, simultaneously, in a relation which cannot suppress excess, play, dislocation, a constant sliding of signified under signifier, and the lack which the imaginary seeks to make good in the first place.

Since Lacan

During the 1970s, particularly in England, a mode of critical thinking was worked out which aimed to consider imaginary and symbolic together in the analysis of cultural texts. Besides a sense of the importance of *subjectivity* in this discussion, there was also a determination to hold onto awareness of formal, *semiological* features. Further, it was affirmed that the particular operation of symbolic and imaginary introduced an *ideological* force.

This brave synthesis (or would-be synthesis) could not be sustained. In the period since then the trajectory of interest (interests) in critical theory and textual analysis has changed, for a number of reasons I shall touch on more fully in another section. Class politics, as supported by a Marxist theory of ideology, were not just supplemented but replaced by other forms of politics. The influence of Lacan, Althusser and Barthes declined and gave way to that of Derrida, Deleuze and others. The presence and absence Lacan discerned in the play between symbolic and imaginary was completely redefined and reorganised as a contrast between presence and difference, the 'metaphysics' of presence and the 'dissemination' of difference. It would be mistaken to try to lay blame for this at the door of any particular writer, since it emerges in a much wider field of cultural forces, which were often heading not towards a specific text but away from it.

I am prepared to read these developments as consequences, or symptoms, or simply what is liable to happen if Lacan's distinction between imaginary and symbolic becomes overlaid. Very schematically at this juncture, I would anticipate four associated lines of divergence from the privileging of difference.

One is the *flight from the imaginary* already implied. Another might be termed *signified for signifier*, since the contrast between imaginary and symbolic threw massive emphasis on the operation of the signifier and so on the 'forms' in which meaning is realised. So also does an application of the contrast between *enunciation* and *enounced*. Although Marxism *au pied de la lettre* became dissipated, the *utopianism* written into the Marxist problematic of class politics continued, but was relocated in other expressions, other ideas of politics. The notion of ideology thought by some theorists of the 1970s to be inscribed in subjectivity underwent two transformations, first into subjectivity as itself a mode of politics, and then into a certain *effacement of subjectivity* altogether.

I shall not attempt a comprehensive theoretical justification of this position. Rather, I shall give a close reading of a number of examples which in different ways may illustrate and clarify it.

2   Heath

In 1931 Ezra Pound remarked that 'Anything that happens to mind in England has usually happened somewhere else first' (1954: 30). During the 1960s something did happen to mind in England. The 'New Left', associated with the journal *New Left Review*, took over and promoted the Marxism of Louis Althusser, together with his rationalist method, which the New Left tried to inject into the empiricism of the native tradition.

Screen

Around 1970 a small subgroup of the New Left began to develop work in the area of art and aesthetic practice, taking cinema as its example. The vehicle for this intervention was the film journal *Screen*, and work in it became a collective endeavour, with a number of people playing off each other. At the same time exciting new names were crossing the Channel every month.

Taking on board Althusser's notion of a series of practices, including ideological practice (which itself includes cinema), as relatively autonomous, *Screen* did not engage in what it denigrated as 'content analysis', but concentrated on film as a specific practice, what Heath described as its 'ideological *operation*' (italics original) (Heath 1981: 53). The project was to theorise 'the encounter of Marxism and psychoanalysis on the terrain of semiotics' (Heath 1976), to think cinema as simultaneously determined semiologically, ideologically and subjectively.

Screen envisages the ideological operation of film as affording a position for the subject. This view leans on the work of Julia Kristeva, whose *Revolution in Poetic Language* (published in French in 1974) affirms that the 'realm of signification' is always 'a realm of *positions* . . . establishing the *identification* of the subject' (1984: 43). Kristeva gives a history of literary texts analysed in terms of subject and position; in contrast *Screen*, following Althusser's argument that the subject is constituted by being 'hailed' or 'interpellated' into ideology (1977: 121–73), conceives positionality as an effect of the text on its *reader*.

What is formally specific to film is a textual organisation of vision. Putting this at the forefront of attention led the *Screen* collective towards Lacan's discussion in *Seminar 11* of the relation between the gaze and perspective representation in the graphic art of the Quattrocento (Lacan 1977b: 65–119). Here Lacan says, 'That which is light looks at me' (96): if there is light, I can see – but I can also be seen. Vision, then, is the condition for someone else to look at me, a point of view from which I myself can never see, since it belongs to the Other: 'I see only from one point, but in my existence I am looked at from all sides' (72). To 'see the world' comes within the dominion of the conscious I, the imaginary; to 'be the object of the gaze' represents the operation of the unconscious, the domain of the symbolic on which I depend but which I can never lay claim to.

'Narrative Space'

Arguably, the *Screen* project comes nearest to realisation in an essay on 'Narrative Space' by Stephen Heath, published in 1976. Here, as elsewhere, I shall be obliged to give a summary of this account, with cited extracts, before moving to any comments or criticism.

Heath particularly analyses 'classical cinema', that is, conventional, realist cinema. From its invention, what had struck audiences was the apparent realism of the medium, so that, as Heath says, the assumption was easily made that 'the space of film is the space of reality' (1981: 25). His premise is that any such match between film and world is 'a matter of representation', of 'discourse' and 'the organisation of images' (26). Moreover, that representation, that organisation, Heath argues, is historically distinctive, rooted in Quattrocento space, quoting Francastel:

> Spaces are born and die like societies; they live, they have a history. In the fifteenth century, the human societies of Western Europe organised, in the material and intellectual senses of the term, a space completely different from that of the preceding generations.
>
> (cited Heath 1981: 29)

We might want to think of this homogeneously continuous space as classical space.

Developed to depict three-dimensional objects on a flat surface, Quattrocento space relies not only on linear perspective, but also on various strategies for fixing the viewer at the centre of an apparently all-embracing view. It is a strength of Heath's account that he acknowledges such placing as an ideal rather than something consistently achieved: there are always deviations, which uphold the norm by being subordinated to it, just as in tonic music variation in fact supports the tonic or keynote. Quattrocento space is the condition for photography (most photography), and photography in turn is the ground for cinema. Such space, at once graphic, photographic and cinematic, can offer a world 'conceived outside of process and practice, empirical scene of the confirmed and central master-spectator' (31). In realist cinema it is as though the eye is 'free from the body' (32).

But there is a difficulty. Unlike painting and photography, cinema consists of 'moving pictures'. Process and movement constantly threaten the fixity and centring aimed for by the Western tradition of the still image. If figures move, they may remind the spectator of the blank absence which frames the screen like the frame of a picture. Editing makes transitions between shots, which again introduces mobility of a different kind. Cinema has responded by developing two procedures: one is to reactivate the Quattrocento system for organising composition within the frame; the other is to edit cuts to create the story-line.

Hence what Heath terms 'narrative space': the attempt to make good a dangerous instability through a narrativisation which 'contains the mobility that could threaten the clarity of vision' (36). The narrative space of classic cinema constantly renews a centred perspective for the spectator, converting 'seen into scene' and thus holding 'signifier on signified' (37), minimising the distinction between the world of the fiction and reality, a 'difference' which, in Heath's words, 'is the term of an ultimate similarity' (41). For example, the beginning of *Jaws*:

> a beach party with the camera tracking slowly right along the line of the faces of the participants until it stops on a young man looking off; eyeline cut to a young woman who is thus revealed as the object of his gaze; cut to a high-angle shot onto the party that shows its general

> space, its situation, before the start of the action with the run down to
> the ocean and the first shark attack.   (41)

Everything advised by conventional film manuals – use of master-
shot, the 180-degree rule, matching on action, eyeline matching,
avoidance of 'impossible angles' – is designed to ensure that '"the
spectator's illusion of seeing a continuous piece of action is not inter-
rupted"' (cited by Heath from a book on film editing: 42).

It is crucial, however, that 'narration is to be held on the narrated,
the enunciation on the enounced' (43): there is no question of what
has been vaguely referred to as 'transparency', since realist cinema
does not get rid of the signs of production, but rather 'contains them'
within a process of narrativisation (as I will suggest, this point is much
more than technical). Heath instances style and genre as means for
containing excess, following on from his claim that the Quattrocento
regime is an ideal rather than a simple actualisation. Norman Bryson
has shown how, even in such a classical image as Masaccio's *Trinity*,
which is in Santa Maria Novella in Florence, there are two vanishing
points, one centred on the figure of the Madonna in the left foreground, but another, the dominant, organised around the body of
Jesus on the Cross (1983: 108–10).

Freud states that every 'finding of an object [of desire] is in fact a
refinding of it' (1977: 145). Stephen Heath proposes that the implication of the spectator subject in realist film is 'a constant refinding'
continued between loss and (would-be) making good:

> In its movement, its framings, its cuts, its intermittences, the film
> ceaselessly poses an absence, a lack, which is ceaselessly recaptured
> for – one needs to be able to say 'forin' – the film, that process
> binding the spectator as subject in the realisation of the film's space.
> (1981: 52)

There is 'a perpetual retotalisation of the imaginary' consequent upon
the '"initial" production of the subject in the symbolic order' (53), a
process of enunciation instating the very lack the imaginary would
recapture. Narrativisation is the term of a 'film's entertaining' (62) in
the etymological sense by which 'entertainment' is a holding in.

Heath and after

Except in certain rather specialised areas of film theory, Heath's analysis of 'narrative space' is not now well known. The moment in culture which at the time made it possible and exhilarating has passed, the moment of the counter-culture which trailed in its wake an alternative sense of cinema exemplified in the practice of directors such as Brakhage, Godard, Oshima and Straub-Huillet (all alluded to in 'Narrative Space'). This intervention made visible the heavy weight of convention lying over mainstream cinema. Teaching film today, I notice that students, at least in England, have no tolerance whatsoever for any movie which is not immediately entertaining.

In its detailed illustration of formal features, 'Narrative Space' bears considerable empirical force. It specifically addresses that interest with reference to the distinction between enunciation and enounced, showing how narration seeks to hold 'enunciation on enounced' (54). And although the essay does offer itself as metalanguage – able to understand mainstream cinematic representation better than it generally understands itself – this stance is unsettled by the text's *own* process of enunciation. I have not had space to discuss the examples – particularly the long passage on Hitchcock's *Suspicion* which opens the piece and that on Oshima's *Death by Hanging* which closes it. An all-encompassing linear order of exposition is avoided, while its own stylistic texture shows a certain preference for parataxis over syntaxis, the juxtaposition of terms in lists, rather than closure through subordination.

Heath's analysis of narrative space is pervaded by the concept of subjectivity. Drawing on the Lacanian distinction between imaginary and symbolic, it is able to suggest how, as an organisation of the symbolic, narrative space is constructed for specific imaginary effects. And this undeviating emphasis includes an explanation of why this cinematic effect yields enjoyment for the viewer. In another essay Heath discriminates between the three 'looks' of cinema:

(1)   the look of the camera at what is represented 'within' the movie;
(2)   the look of the spectator at the screen;
(3)   the look of characters at people and things they can see.

(1981: 119)

To narrativise space is to invite the viewing subject into identification with a position of coherent and unified vision, and into the narcissistic pleasures that go with this. The three looks – of the camera, the spectator, individuals on screen – are meant to coincide, as though in seeing what they see, we are shown all there is.

Subjectivity and desire

In film, Heath concludes, the subject 'is held in a shifting and placing of desire' (53), desire which in Lacan's account is always metonymic and which, in the instance of cinema, may be provoked by 'the metonymy as a "taking place"' (46). Lacan states repeatedly that 'desire is the desire of the Other' (for example, 1977a: 264; 1977b: 235), exploiting the ambiguity of the French 'de' ('désire de l'Autre') which covers both desire *for* and desire *from*. It may be plausible to concede that I cannot desire myself, so must enter desire as I am desired – that a baby, for example, should want to be what its mother wants. It's less easy to understand why this principle is active between my look and the gaze of the Other.

As a negative reason, one might think of the radical unease caused by the gaze of the Other, so that any taming of the gaze will go to assuage anxiety. Positively, we may recall that most world religions have imagined a supreme god, or collection of immortals set above space and time, who can see and know everything and everyone. In Milton's *Paradise Lost* even Satan is able to see 'all this world at once' (III: 543). So in the drama of vision, of seeing and being seen, my desire for the Other is realised in the wish to see as the Other sees, escaping the unique point from which I see, and being able to see myself 'in my existence', where 'I am looked at from all sides' (Lacan 1977b: 72). Narrative space excites this desire and contrives to respond to it.

Narrative space does not offer transparency, but rather contains the excess arising from the transitions of 'moving' pictures. To suppose any means of representation could actually be transparent is to assume a subject given prior to its production and inclusion within language, discourse and representation. In an article not reprinted, Heath summarises an alternative conception: that the subject is always located, produced and reproduced in history:

it is not, in other words, that there is first of all the construction of a

subject for social/ideological formations and then the placing of that
constructed subject-support in those formations, it is that the two
processes are one, in a kind of necessary simultaneity – like the recto
and verso [front and back] of a piece of paper.   (1976–7: 62)

He gives a radical reading to Lacan's assertion that the signifier represents a subject for another signifier. The subject of 'Narrative Space'
does not exist outside the sum of discourses and representations of
which it is a variable effect. The subject produces narrative space
while simultaneously being produced by it; narrative space is the
(local) condition of the subject's possibility. So a cinematic spectator
is 'cut in as a subject' to a process of vision, in 'a positioning and positioned movement' (1981: 27).

On the question of the subject, it might be urged that Heath, writing
in 1976, follows Althusser a little too closely. Whatever conviction the
analysis of Quattrocento space and cinematic narrative space imports
via Lacanian psychoanalysis, it is not obvious that such a visual
regime extends from subjectivity directly onto the ground of what is
usually thought of as historical and ideological. This doubt is not
entirely laid to rest by Heath's claims that 'cinema is not simply and
specifically ideological' (33) or that 'ideological representation'
supports itself from the 'production of the subject in the symbolic
order' (53). Elsewhere Heath accepts that neither 'the imaginary' nor
'the symbolic is . . . reducible to the ideological' (1981: 105). Yet at
times 'Narrative Space' suggests an almost Heideggerian enthusiasm
for the view that the history of subjectivity is an almost complete
history which includes ideology, and this is why it insists on joining
'the crucial role of psychoanalysis, as potential science of the
construction of the subject, with historical materialism' (53).

Again, despite its thesis that the subject is active in positioning
itself, as well as being positioned, 'Narrative Space' could be charged
with promoting a structuralism in which the text constructs its viewer
as a passive effect, so that a description of the text comprehends a
description of someone's response to it. Two replies can be given to
this. One is that Heath's analysis makes a full place for resistance,
emphasising the struggle of the text to contain the desire which it also
causes, and which always threatens to exceed any measurable effect.
Another would be along the lines that, whatever individual texts may
or may not lead to in specific viewers and readers, 'Narrative Space' is
considering a massive and long-term visual regime originating in the

Italian Renaissance of the fifteenth century, an institution which could be named as epochal.

I don't believe that is the end of the issue of text-and-response at all. But it may be important to defend the position Heath occupies, that, as Lapsley and Westlake argue in *Film Theory: An Introduction*, 'the subject is at once the producer and the product of meaning' (1988: 53). Failure to take this view on board entails two corresponding limitations for any attempt at a political interpretation of the aesthetic. If the subject is wholly determined by the text, meaning is fixed once and for all, and that's it; if the subject makes the text, then there is no point at all in discussing texts. It is therefore hard to see how serious interpretation can proceed except on the basis of Heath's statement that there is a 'dialectic of the subject' (1976–7: 50) in the relation between reader and text.

In looking for political alternatives to narrative space, Heath stands at some distance from conventional notions of the avant-garde. Significantly, it is exactly his belief that the imaginary givens of institutions, systems of representation and texts are defined only to be gone beyond that conducts the account to an anti-utopian stance. What he refers to as 'an aesthetics of transgression' (and which, showing how little he has been reading Derrida, he names as 'deconstruction') quickly reveals itself as caught in 'the impasse of formal device'. Instead, he recommends work not from any position 'beyond' (which is in any case impossible), but at the limits of the imaginary, and on the construction of meaning 'in a specific signifying practice in a given socio-historical situation' (1981: 64). These are lessons that since 1976 have been too casually put aside.

3   From Marxism to Difference

When I went to university a few years after the invasion of Hungary, I came across only three Marxists, all members of the Communist Party, all prepared to justify the Soviet action. Who would have guessed then that a generation of Western intellectuals were once again about to embrace Marxism?

Sixties Marxism surfed in on the waves of the counter-culture, and it would require a separate book to begin to consider in detail the ramifications of this effect. Here I want to give a preliminary outline and set out a proposal: that this version of Marxism succeeded as well as it did because it imported with it not just utopian energies, but also a critique of the subject; and that the fading of historical materialism as an intellectual force bequeathed a continuing preoccupation with forms of subjectivity, as well as a residue of the utopian impulse.

There is a scene in Alex Cox's film *Sid and Nancy* (1986) in which a line of punks sit on a wall muttering, and one of them says, 'I hate fuckin' hippies.' I do know that a younger generation is just not very interested in the arguments within Marxism which seemed so important two decades ago, but I would ask for some patience here. You cannot come to grips with much of critical theory written since 1980 without appreciating the Marxist legacy it secretes.

Classic Marxism

Is it possible to recapitulate classic Marxism in three principles? A first would be that, when Hegel thought spirit or mind determined its real-isation in the finite world, he stood reality on its head and, as Marx said, 'it must be turned right side up again' (Marx and Engels 1950: I, 414), so that materialism is put first. Second, in a dialectical relation between subject and object, the human species, through labour, in its struggle with nature produces its means of subsistence and simultaneously itself.

But third, the relation between subject and object can become alienated from itself, and in fact it has, for 'the history of all hitherto-existing society is the history of class struggles' (I: 33). Class struggle is caused by alienation, when a ruling class, through a form of private ownership and control, appropriates the fruits of collective human labour for itself, as is now the case with the capitalist class and the working class. Eradicate capitalism, organise the working class into the ruling class, expropriate the expropriators – and 'pre-history' will come to an end, as class antagonism is superseded in a conflict-free communist utopia.

Under public ownership, so the story goes, alienation of subject and object is transformed into free expression. 'Production based on exchange value breaks down', use will replace the commodity, with labour reduced to a minimum, and all this 'corresponds to the artistic, scientific etc. development of the individuals in the time set free, and with the means created, for all of them' (Marx 1973: 705–6). In this future you will hunt in the morning, fish in the afternoon, rear cattle in the evening and criticise after dinner 'without ever becoming hunter, fisherman, cowherd or critic' (Marx 1977: 169).

Since *Capital* was published in 1867, the number of questions put to classic Marxism has accumulated. Has the main form of collectivity been economic class (as Marx anticipated) or nation? Does a single master-narrative comprehend the totality of human history? Can you really run a modern economy through centralised state control, as in the two remaining examples of applied Marxism, Cuba and North Korea? Is it the case that classic Marxism is functionalist in citing the actual consequences of behaviour as though these were intended, but without 'demonstrating that it has *beneficial* consequences for someone or something' (Elster 1985: 27)?

Each of the three principles sketched earlier can be objected to. Whether in Hegel's inversion, or turned the right way up by Marx, any such opposition as 'materialism/idealism' cannot be sustained. Second, Marx's privileging of production through labour overlooks the at least equal importance in the life of the human species of sexual reproduction and all that generally entails. Third, the 'alienation' of subject and object seems to be inherent and not a passing contingency. If, as Jacques Derrida remarks succinctly, 'Immediacy is derived' (1976: 157), if the presence of an object to a subject is always a mirage, their alienation from each other cannot be annealed by any communist utopia.

Althusser, Derrida and Marxism

During the 1960s the work of the French Communist Party intellectual, Louis Althusser, went some way to meet difficulties of this kind. In what was arguably an act of deconstruction *avant la lettre*, he took the distinction which may be summarised as that between 'materialism' and 'idealism' and showed that, whichever term you used to denigrate the other, it was in fact a binary opposition which *itself* had to be rejected (for this see particularly the 1962 essay 'Contradiction and Overdetermination', Althusser 1969: 87–128). Althusser rethought Marx's spatial view – that social being determines consciousness – as a temporality, a number of co-existing practices (notably economic, political and ideological) which developed in time, according to their own specific materiality, but in relation to each other.

However, Althusser retained a concept of economic determination, in a somewhat refined form, by claiming that economic practice determined 'in the last instance' which of the various practices was dominant in any conjuncture. He qualified this by claiming further that no one would ever actually see economic practice exerting this determination, for 'the lonely hour of the "last instance" never comes' (1969: 113). Marx liked to point out that, judging from appearance, people imagine the sun goes round the earth, while the scientific truth is that really the earth goes round the sun (see for example Marx and Engels 1950: I, 384); Althusser took the position that 'theoretical practice', defined as a process that takes place within knowledge (1969: 161–218), could provide an account of the social formation which was scientific; this meant developing theory was as much a work of class struggle as anything that happened on a factory floor.

In an interview of 1989 Jacques Derrida notes that he and Althusser found they had it in common that they came from Algeria; Althusser supported Derrida's application for a post with him at the Ecole Normale Supérieure and they were colleagues for 20 years. It should not have come as too much of a surprise that Derrida defended Marxism in some lectures in 1993, nor that he should extend some of Althusser's criticisms. For anyone who has ever been a Marxist it is unsettling to watch the pillars go down one after another, as they do

in *Specters of Marx* (1994a). No binary opposition between materialism and idealism can be sustained:

> Marx does not like ghosts any more than his adversaries do. He does
> not want to believe in them. But he thinks of nothing else. He believes
> rather in what is supposed to distinguish them from actual reality,
> living effectivity. He believes he can oppose them, like life to death,
> like vain appearances of the simulacrum to real presence.
>
> (Derrida 1994a: 46–7)

The associated opposition between use-value and exchange-value is
breached (161–2). Any notion of class as a 'self-identity' is suspended,
as is all sense of 'the determination of the superstructure as idea' (55).
Difficulties ensue from Althusser's attempt to repair Marx's concept
of economic determination, as Derrida indicates in the interview,
alluding to Althusser when he asks what it means to appeal to 'the last
instance', if the last instance never appears as such. He urges that we
refer instead to a Heideggerian account of Being-under-erasure. Of
course in the mid-1960s you could not do this and remain a member
of the French Communist Party.

Derrida stands entirely apart from any Marxist opposition between
the real and the apparent which would support the logic of a science
opposed to the falsity of ideology. Marxism is not defended for its
truth, but rather for its effectiveness, because it maintains the
promise of democracy within a non-religious systematic discourse:
'Whether they wish it or know it or not, all men and women, all over
the Earth, are today to a certain extent the heirs of Marx and Marxism'
(1994a: 91). However, a major reason why Marxism managed to establish itself all over the earth after 1867 was that people believed it was
true; one may wonder how long, how effectively, a Marxism can keep
going stripped of any claim to scientificity. At the end of *Specters of
Marx* Derrida calls for the foundation of a new International, though
this has not happened.

The legacy of Marxism in critical theory

During the 1970s intellectual Marxism in the West began to fade. I am
not aware of any event, any publication, any specific debate at which
the light started to change, though I do recall a conference in London

in 1976 when doubts about Althusser's opposition between science and ideology was the main topic of informal discussion.

Althusserian Marxism left a determining residue for so-called 'critical theory'. The classic Marxist notion of labour and production had been supplemented in Althusser by a corresponding emphasis on reproduction. Traditional humanist Marxism was fairly consistently hostile to any view of subjectivity other than that it was an effect of class position. Althusser aimed to make good this weakness, and in 1964 contributed an essay on 'Freud and Lacan', which justified psychoanalysis as a science with its own object (the unconscious), and insisted that it was a way of theorising what is referred to as 'the extraordinary adventure' which 'transforms a small animal conceived by a man and a woman into a small human child' (1977: 189).

The essay on ideology of 1969 opens its argument by referring to Marx's pronouncement that the social formation reproduces the conditions of production. This is now extended to cover the reproduction not only of productive forces but of 'labour power', which in turn requires reproduction of subjects who submit to 'the ruling ideology for workers' (1977: 128). On this basis Althusser proposes that ideology carries out its defining function in '"*constituting concrete individuals as subjects*"' (160), subjects, that is, who imagine they are free from ideology, who '"work by themselves"' (169) and, precisely in that seeming freedom, display themselves as an effect of ideological construction.

During the 1970s and early 1980s, in what I would want to name as 'British poststructuralism', an Althusserian critique of the subject seeded itself across the human sciences: in historical studies (Perry Anderson and Tom Nairn); sociology (Barry Hindess and Paul Hirst); cultural studies (the Birmingham Centre for Contemporary Cultural Studies); film (*Screen*); literary criticism (Raymond Williams and Terry Eagleton); social psychology (the group around the journal *Ideology and Consciousness*); art history (Norman Bryson and Griselda Pollock); musicology (Alan Durant).

It would be quite wrong to think that these consequences occurred outside a larger field of discursive forces. Modernism, like its contemporary, psychoanalysis, circled around a crisis over subjectivity; and, as usually happens, the practice of writers and artists was not properly reflected at the level of theoretical concern until a generation later (Jacques Lacan's connections with Surrealism are well known). In 1916 Ezra Pound wrote that,

> In the 'search for oneself' . . . one gropes, one finds some seeming
> verity. One says 'I am' this, that or the other, and with the words
> scarcely uttered one ceases to be that thing.   (1960: 85)

It is evident that these questions around the dispersed subject resur-
faced in a radical context with the counter-culture of the Vietnam
years.

Althusserian Marxism did not take root in the United States.
Instead, a rather more extreme and Romantic version of humanism
experienced the impact of American 'deconstruction', influenced
particularly by Paul de Man, and associated with Derrida, rather than
Althusser or Lacan. The effects were not dissimilar, at least when any
notion of a binary structure privileging 'presence' was severely criticised.

With traditional Marxism suspended and politically radical movements beginning to dissipate, energies were released for other ends. A
preoccupation with subjectivity continued, as did a utopian desire,
but with a mutation in the figure who is treated unjustly. The working
man exploited by capitalism was displaced by other victim subjects in
a kind of metonymic series – a woman oppressed by patriarchy, a
member of an ethnic minority or a colonial people, a gay person
subjected to homophobia. How far these changes originated in the
preceding intellectual and cultural formation can be judged by, for
example, the extraordinary ease with which *Screen* was transformed,
in no more than two years after the publication of Laura Mulvey's
article 'Visual Pleasure and Narrative Cinema' in 1975, from a
predominantly Marxist to a predominantly feminist journal. Realist
film was now read as construing 'Woman as image, man as bearer of
the look' (Mulvey 1992: 162) in a visual regime which the modernist
text threw into question.

I would not want to be misunderstood in reporting any of this.
Important political gains were made, many long overdue. But at the
same time a certain price was paid. To be quite clear: my proposal is
that, as other definitions of identity came to supplant class as a focus
of struggle, the utopian impulse showed itself in the way a typical
question was typically answered. How can there be identity which
does not disparage and deny the other which that same identity
produces along with itself? Too often the reply was phrased not
so much in these terms, but as a willingness to surrender any possible

account of identity as presence, in favour of a privileging of difference. Before developing this I want to make an appropriate digression.

The signifier

Utopianism is a remainder of Marxism. And it is accompanied by a retreat from the signifier. One of the things that's happened since Heath published 'Narrative Space' in 1976 is that fans of theory have stopped reading linguistics, mainly, I suspect, for political reasons – the dismissal of '*mere* formalism'.

Not everyone was keen on linguistics, semiotics, semiology, structuralism, even in the 1970s. Now, Saussure is still read but with an eye to difference and the differential operation of the phoneme. The distinction between *langue* and *parole*, embodying the principle that where there is an effect there must be a system, is set aside, as is the contrast between syntagmatic and paradigmatic axes (the linguistic support for Lacan's argument that coherent discourse develops as an effect in the subject of temporary closure in the syntagmatic chain). A number of key texts in linguistics get ignored: Jakobson's distinction between enunciation and enounced and their two subjects (1971), his essay on poetics and linguistics (1960); Benveniste's crucial distinction between the language and discourse, which regards utterance up to the level of the sentence as the province of language, while with anything beyond that, the stringing together of sentences, 'we leave the domain of language as a system of signs and enter into another universe . . . whose expression is discourse' (1971: 110). Are people still reading Roland Barthes? I suspect not, which means they are not familiar with the analysis of the visual image in terms of first and second order signification (see 1972: 113–17), nor with his pathbreaking 'Introduction to the Structural Analysis of Narratives' (1977: 79–124).

There are reasons for this neglect, if that is what it is. Limits to the formalist analysis became obvious the moment the questions of politics, history and ideology were posed, as they were from 1968 (and I would note that some well-versed critics couldn't – or wouldn't – make the transition, like Frank Kermode, for instance). Formalism must consider the text as closed, effect of an apparently self-sufficient system, so bypassing the historical positioning of text and reader (in a sense such formalism always worked better for texts in a larger regime, as does 'Narrative Space', or Umberto Eco's dazzling structuralist account of the James Bond novels, see 1979: 144–72). But that is not the end of the matter, a satisfactory political reason to reject formalist analysis. For with the flight into content analysis, the deeper structures of meaning get casually disregarded, the sense of meaning produced for the reader, not just by what a text says but by the operation of the signifier, what the text *does*. As Barthes says, 'a little formalism turns one away from History, but . . . a lot brings one back to it' (1972: 112). The reason is that history is most indelibly inscribed in textuality at the level of the signifier. Go far enough with that, Barthes suggests, and you are driven round to history and politics.

A preliminary example: gender and difference

In 1982 a correspondence between Christie V. McDonald and Jacques Derrida was published in *Diacritics* with the title 'Choreographies', Derrida's replies being translated by McDonald (Derrida 1995a: 89–108). McDonald begins by asking Derrida to respond to Emma Goldman's nice assertion that 'If I can't dance I don't want to be part of your revolution' (89). In response, Derrida speculates that Goldman in her idea of a long dance may have had in mind 'a completely other history', one of 'paradoxical laws and non-dialectical discontinuities, a history of absolutely heterogeneous pockets, irreducible particularities, of unheard-of and incalculable sexual differences' (93). This line of thought brings Derrida round to asking, 'Must one think "difference" "before" sexual difference or taking off "from" it?' (98), a line of thought which he draws away from any definition of what is 'specifically feminine' towards Heidegger and his unequivocal assertion that 'the *Dasein is neuter*' (104).

Elaborating this assertion, Derrida states that it does not signify 'the absence of sexuality', but rather 'the absence of any mark belonging to one of the two sexes', a view he further develops in the claim that '*Dasein* as *Dasein* does not carry with it the mark of this opposition (or alternative) between the two sexes' (104). Pressed again on the question of 'the dance', he warns that he is approaching a 'shadowy area', but remarks that he has felt the necessity for what he terms 'a choreographic text with polysexual signatures'. From 'opposition (or alternative)' he moves to the idea of 'a certain dissymmetry' as the law of sexual difference, a dissymmetry he qualifies as 'doubly unilaterally inordinate, like a kind of reciprocal respective and respectful exces-siveness' (107).

It is with this set of questions and comments that Derrida frames what has become a famous question and famous answer. The ques-tion he asks himself is, 'what if we were to approach here (for one does not arrive at this as one would at a determined location) the area of a relationship to the other where the code of sexual marks would no longer be discriminating?' (108). The reply is as follows:

> The relationship would not be a-sexual, far from it, but would be sexual otherwise; beyond the binary difference that governs the decorum of all codes, beyond the opposition feminine/masculine, beyond bisexuality as well, beyond homosexuality and heterosexual-ity which come to the same thing. As I dream of saving the chance that this question offers, I would like to believe in the multiplicity of sexually marked voices. I would like to believe in the masses, this indeterminable number of blended voices, this mobile of non-identi-fied sexual marks whose choreography can carry, divide, multiply the body of each 'individual', whether he be classified as 'man' or 'woman' according to the criteria of usage.   (108)

I do not intend to add to this, except to note two things. Clearly Derrida is stepping away from a notion of sexual difference as a binary opposition, in which masculine is presupposed as a norm or presence, in relation to which feminine may be denigrated as its outside, its other, merely a term to support its privilege. And, as clearly, his tone in even formulating this question and possible response is tentative in the extreme. Stating that he has 'felt the necessity for a chorus, a choreographic text', he goes on to say that he 'has a dream of saving the chance that this question offers' and that it lies in the direction of what he 'would like to believe in'.

An issue of *boundary 2* in 1984 published another correspondence with Derrida, 'Voice II', now with Verena Andermatt Conley (she dates her address to him as 31 October 1982 and does the translation herself) (Derrida 1995a: 156–70). Conley begins by citing the whole of the passage quoted above, as well as some additional sentences that come before and after it. The questions she puts to it need to be given at length. Invoking 'the multiplicity of sexually marked voices', Conley asks:

Where do these voices traverse? In what region which cannot be reduced to a precise locus? Of what kind of voices is it a question? Do they have 'attachments' to some specific point? Are they voices of identifiable people or are they unidentifiable? of a multiplicity of 'men' or 'women' one carries within oneself, one's father, mother, son, daughter, all of whom have to be thought of outside of a social role, of course, and other *he's* and *she's*, known or unknown, with whom one is in dialogue and who dialogue in each of us. Does this dialogue take place with the other, with the other of the other or of others, toward a displacement of what you call the number 2, or is it the result of it? – Are these voices linked to pulsions? Would it limit their multiplicity if one advanced the hypothesis of a difference, of differences in libidinal economies which would be, for lack of better things, qualified by traditional adjectives, 'masculine', 'feminine' – adjectives which, at the limit, one should be able to replace with other qualifiers, color adjectives for example?   (Derrida 1995a: 157)

In an important extended footnote to *Three Essays on the Theory of Sexuality* Freud distinguishes 'masculine' and 'feminine' as (1) pertaining to the body, (2) social roles and (3) attributes shaped by unconscious determination, concluding that 'every individual' displays 'a mixture of the character-traits belonging to his own and to the opposite sex' (1977: 141–2). (Having unsettled any necessary coincidence of biological, sociological and psychical identifications with the claim that these are, in fact, always 'mixed', Freud goes on to reinstate a masculinised definition of them as belonging to '*his* own and to the opposite sex', my italics). Conley's very suggestive questions do not seem to concern identity defined by the body, but certainly press Derrida on the issue of identity as social placing ('Are they voices of identifiable people or are they unidentifiable?') and as unconscious determination ('Are these voices linked to pulsions?'). She conforms to Freud's view when she affirms that the qualifiers masculine and feminine do not 'refer in an exclusive way to one or other of the sexes', while accepting that 'one would tend to find a libidinal economy said to be feminine more easily in a woman', for example.

Conley is also interested in how these voices would appear as gendered in artistic practices. She goes on to ask, 'What would be the relation between those multiple voices, the law (of castration) and artistic inscription?' (158). In his response, which takes up the rest of the interview, Derrida does not hesitate to subscribe to the idea of law, agreeing that the 'space' which pre-exists these voices must 'threaten to submit them to its law' (160), thus distancing himself from any reading which might take his earlier reference to 'polysexual signatures' as an invocation of the phase when, according to Freud, children can be 'polymorphously perverse' before submitting to castration (1977: 109).

After this opening move, Derrida advances into what is for him a not unconventional middle game, by setting aside any notion of voice as full presence, in favour of writing. Might we not, he asks, try to think or listen to a voice without presuppositions about the body (the voice of philosophy or science or everyday language), 'to try to speak or to hear voice without reference to a fixed place' (Derrida 1995a: 160)? But we witness the voice detached in this kind of way on 'the telephone, the radio, the record, and so forth'. Detached thus from the body, it becomes 'a trace, a spacing, a writing, but neither a simple presence nor a dispersion of meaning' (161). Which, for Derrida, it always already is.

I have some questions of my own about some of the qualifiers here. Is it possible for us to speak or hear a voice 'without reference to a fixed place', without, that is, reference to any fixed place at all? And do we have to choose between 'a simple presence' and 'dispersion of meaning', or might a complex and relativised 'presence' be admissible, something like that conjured up by Lacan's account of the imaginary? Though directed generally at those who have been more completely persuaded by Derrida's terms than I am, questions pointing in this direction will come up in the examples to be discussed.

'Perhaps', Derrida wonders, 'where there is voice, sex becomes undecided' (161). What appears most strongly to motivate Derrida's line of speculation is a reluctance to endorse 'a system of oppositions' which would assign polyphony 'to one of the marks of the same and very limited binary code', a wariness about going along with a sense of liberation which is, as he says it usually is, 'dominated by values of "person", "self", even of the "body" as referential identity' (163).

Toril Moi

The velleities of what Derrida himself describes as having the 'rebellious force of affirmation' (163) do not facilitate any unambiguous interpretation of his replies to Conley. There is much less difficulty in understanding the reading Toril Moi gives to the cited passage from 'Choreographies' in her book *Sexual/Textual Politics* (1985). At the very end, with the disclaimer that Derrida's utterance is at once 'sibylline and suggestive', Moi concludes the book by citing Derrida's answer to his own question, 'What if we were to approach ... the area of a relationship to the other where the code of sexual marks would no longer be discriminating?' She gives the whole passage from 'The relationship would not be a-sexual . . . ' down to ' "man" or "woman" according to the criteria of usage' (Moi 1985: 172–3; see above p. 25). The context Moi provides for this passage renders it much less sibylline, in one sense of that term, than it was in Derrida's original interview.

Moi's text is refreshingly explicit, decisively argued, conscientious, its theme announced more than once in a vocabulary made familiar by Derrida:

> [Virginia Woolf] understood that the goal of the feminist struggle must precisely be to deconstruct the death-dealing binary opposi-tions of masculinity and femininity.   (13)

Or again:

> it is necessary at once to deconstruct the opposition between tradi-tionally 'masculine' and traditionally 'feminine' values *and* to confront the full political force and reality of such categories.
>
> (160; see also 153–4)

It follows that any writer must be criticised if they affirm a tradition-ally 'masculine' position. But more immediately for Moi's concerns, it also follows that feminist writers, however well intentioned, are to be reproached if they uphold any notion of traditionally 'feminine' iden-tity, since this in turn has the effect of supporting the binary opposi-tion. Accordingly, Moi points out that Gilbert and Gubar in *The Madwoman in the Attic* are committed to the essentialist view that there is such a thing as a 'distinctive female power' (cited Moi 1985: 59). The same interrogation is carried forward to French feminist writers.

Hélène Cixous formally takes the position that terms 'like "mascu-line" and "feminine" themselves imprison us within a binary logic' (cited Moi 1985: 108). However – and I omit the details of the analysis

– Moi argues that there is a slippage in Cixous from 'feminine' to 'female' or 'woman', so that 'her evocations of a specifically female writing' seem 'actively intent on promoting an utterly metaphysical case' (113) ('metaphysical' because it accords with the idea of sexual difference as a binary and founding opposition). Again, in the case of Luce Irigaray, a comparable promotion against her best intentions is criticised: it is said to be 'precisely Irigaray's dilemma' that, having shown how 'femininity has been produced exclusively in relation to the logic of the Same, she falls for the temptation to produce her own positive theory of femininity' (139).

Moi advances this criticism with extra confidence because she has an alternative possibility in mind, that afforded by Julia Kristeva. Praised for her 'uncompromising anti-essentialism' (164), Kristeva is recommended as a staunch opponent of any idea of a specifically female or feminine identity, and is cited as arguing that 'Nothing in women's past or present publications seems to allow us to affirm that there is a feminine writing (*écriture féminine*)' (Moi 1985: 163). Instead of finding in certain kinds of writing unacknowledged traces of identity, Kristeva insists that language and discourse, *signifiance*, is 'a question of positioning' (161).

If Moi's analysis is more or less as I suggest, one might think at this point that she will not be able to bring a book about sexual and textual politics to a positive conclusion. The difficulty has already been foreseen. It is open for Moi to stay with her project of deconstructing any binary opposition between masculine and feminine by following through Kristeva's own logic:

> In a sense, then, Kristeva does not have a theory of 'femininity', and even less of 'femaleness'. What she does have is a theory of marginality, subversion and dissidence. In so far as women are defined as marginal by patriarchy, their struggle can be theorised in the same way as any other struggle against a centralised power structure.
>
> (164)

The problem for Moi will be to sustain this position without letting her own argument conform to the very structure of binary oppositions she denounces, oppositions such as self/other, centre/margin, same/different, unified/heterogeneous. I am not sure she entirely eludes this snag.

The discussion seems to get itself into a rather sticky situation

because it sets up right at the outset a resounding paragraph savaging
what is described as a 'traditional humanism', said to be part of 'patriarchal ideology':

> At its centre is the seamlessly unified self – either individual or collec-
> tive – which is commonly called 'Man'. As Luce Irigaray or Hélène
> Cixous would argue, this integrated self is in fact a phallic self,
> constructed on the model of the self-contained, powerful phallus.
> Gloriously autonomous, it banishes from itself all conflict, contradic-
> tion and ambiguity. In this humanist ideology the self is the *sole*
> *author* of history and of the literary text: the humanist creator is
> potent, phallic and male – God in relation to his world, the author in
> relation to his text.   (Moi 1985: 8)

This cuts several corners. Can the individual self be equated so readily
with the collective self? How would one move from 'the integrated
self' to 'a phallic self' (and what is 'a phallic self'?)? Would this humanist self ever succeed in its ascribed aim of banishing from itself all
conflict, without evidence of this victory contaminating its unity?

For the purposes of the present argument, what needs especially to
be remarked is that this notion of the 'seamlessly unified' and 'glori-
ously autonomous' self is apparently the only one on offer. Other
theoretical resources might have been called for at this point, which
would not have entailed a stark choice between a version of identity
as completely (and successfully) unified and autonomous, on the one
hand, and no possibility of 'the self' at all, on the other. Against this
alternative, one could readily distinguish a notion of the ego according to how it may think of itself (autonomous, unified and so on) from
the ego as an effect which is constructed. Descartes, in his account of
the *cogito*, was willing to identify thinking with being; but one does
not have to look far to discover criticisms of the unreflecting dexterity
of the Cartesian 'link between the transparency of the transcendental
subject and his existential affirmation' (Lacan 1977a: 164; see also
1977b: 140–1, 221–7). We do not have to concur with the way the self
or the ego or the subject may think about itself; but we do have to
have an account of individual identity as necessary and inescapable.

The price Moi's argument pays for not distinguishing between
different possibilities for identity might be classified as a Hegelianism
in reverse. For she substantiates an opposition between the bad self of
'traditional humanism' and – via the rejection of essentialism – a good

other made up by 'marginality, subversion and dissidence'. But, one may ask, how radically does this position differ from the traditional account of women as the other of a supposedly masculine sameness? How exactly does this advance a feminist sexual politics? If it is accepted that 'a centralised power structure', equated with both 'patriarchy' and the self of traditional humanism, defines women as marginal, then presumably there can be no position – or identity? – for women other than here. Surely this is a noose you don't have to put your head into?

Nevertheless, it is this kind of unreliable and doubtful opposition which supports Moi's conclusion with Derrida, one enforced by several unhappy and unnecessary options. Kristeva is endorsed once again because of 'her radical deconstruction of the identity of the subject', which provides 'an anti-humanist, anti-essentialist perspective' (172). Does this deconstruction of identity mean the disappearance of identity altogether? Through Kristeva's discussion, 'the hierarchical closure imposed on meaning and language has been opened up to the free play of the signifier' (172). But is a rigidly hierarchical closure the only closure ever available? And is the signifier ever free, entirely free, in its play?

That is the context into which the passage from 'Choreographies' is inserted. It tends to make it hard to interpret Derrida except as inviting us into a free world of difference defined by its opposition to transcendental sameness and identity. In its political connotations it also bears with it a heavy utopian inflection. Moi refers to Derrida's utterance as 'sibylline'. The ancient world knew many sibyls, women inspired usually by Apollo into oracular pronouncement and prophecy. The way Moi reads Derrida's words may render them more sibylline in that sense than they are.

After Marxism

Having suggested, albeit in an abbreviated form, that even if the Marxism of the 1960s and 1970s came to fade, its utopian aspiration survived, like the smile of the Cheshire cat, imprinted in post-Marxist critical writings, I shall go on to broach some discriminations within the work which follows. But I do not want for one moment to give the impression that, in hesitating before some of the arguments that have been made in the tracks of Marxism, especially around utopianism and subjectivity, I have forgotten the large areas of necessary and compelling agreement which form a progressive matrix uniting, however unevenly, the critical writings discussed.

To be crudely explicit, there is a welcome and necessary acceptance that progressive theoretical work can only go forward on the assumption that certain boundaries have been and will stay broken. In different ways, I suppose, these could be understood according to the old Marxist opposition between idealism and materialism. There is, then, a very satisfactory degree of consensus now on three things.

(1)   Descartes's foundationalist opposition between the mind and body, and with it any notion of the 'Cartesian ego' or 'subject' cannot be sustained. Who could ever say where body ends and mind begins?

(2)   The reliance of a theory of knowledge on an absolute opposition between subject and object has gone, between, that is, a knowing subject and an exterior object which is known. Who, except a supernatural deity, could ever be in a position to say where knowledge, subjectivity and discourse ends, and the exteriority of an exterior object begins? Default of this position does not, of course, entail that there is no knowledge of objects *at all.*

(3)   For similar reasons, no one could say where and how far they, their thinking and their very horizon of understanding are situated within history and constructed by history. What may hold this view in some coherence with the previous assertions is recognition that speaking subjects are inside the world. Heidegger says, 'a worldless subject' does not exist (1962: 144); as Jim Morrison sings, 'into this world we're thrown'.

Theory surfing

The 1970s were an exhilarating time for those who had indeed crossed the river and gone into the trees. Whatever particular texts may have helped you break through to the other side, each month, it seemed, brought new imports from Paris: Althusser and Barthes, Lacan and Foucault, Derrida and Deleuze, Cixous, Irigaray, Kristeva. (In the United States, the sequence was significantly different, due to de

Man's promotion of Derrida.) This produced its own structure, for each new writer seemed to require a revision and rethinking of their predecessors.

In part, this is due to the French rationalist tradition of the *essai*, which requires that you dismiss everyone else in order to make a space for yourself. Unused to this, the 'Anglo-Saxons' were shaken into a new practice of reading according to what might be thought a novel temporality, a time 'beyond', a time of non-repetition. However, we should recognise the impact of a 'long wave' effect, in so far as modernity itself is structured around a permanent sense of crisis. In cultural terms, Mario Praz, notably in *The Romantic Agony* (1933), has traced the logic by which Romanticism, in pursuit of the other, was driven to seek ever more unconventional, bizarre and perverse experiences: faster, higher, further. This asymptotic curve was blocked when modernism denied subjectivity as self-possessed *individual* experience, thus associating itself with a more explicit collective politics, and in many cases with the avant-garde (which may be of the left or the right). I would argue that, however we identify the intellectual movement that took place in France in the 1960s, poststructuralism or whatever, it is appropriately seen as the theoretical wing of modernism, a wing on the owl of Minerva.

Recent theory looks back to these antecedents in its sometimes almost apocalyptic and scorched-earth determination to 'make it new' all over. In the following, both from 1977, we should detect the tones of a confident avant-garde. First, from the 'Editorial' of the first issue of *Ideology and Consciousness*:

> In the paper we have attempted to mark out a site for the development of a materialist theory of ideology. . . . This site is partly . . . obscured by various theories . . . which claim to have covered the ground already. We have attempted to make clear why we reject these claims and why the theory which we want to construct cannot merely displace existing theories without replacing their objects.   (1977: 3)

And this is from the 'Introduction' to a reader of articles from the film journal *Screen*:

> Before the Spring of 1971, *Screen's* approach to the problems of screen education had been pragmatic. . . . The new approach . . . rejected this work in favour of a project of the 'development and criti-

cism of theoretical ideas'. It aimed to establish a theoretical foundation for the development of film study, rather than treating education
as simply the 'teaching' of already established critical views.

(Ellis 1977: v)

These gestures, demanding not displacement but replacement, and
something new to establish a foundation for what is to be developed,
are performative acts, recording what *will have been* the case by
'producing the event in the very act of recounting it' (Derrida 1991:
206). Tame though they may now seem, they illustrate the peculiar
necessity for each intervention in critical theory to banish its predecessors and start again from the top.

   This institutionalisation of the moment of rupture repeats itself as
endless self-surpassing: not Lévi-Strauss but Althusser, not Althusser
but Lacan, not Lacan but Derrida . . . not Foucault, Kristeva, Lyotard,
Said, but Bhabha and Butler, not Bhabha and Butler but. . . . A plain
consequence, one I'd like to deflect, is that useful – politically useful –
ideas and explanations get casually forgotten. So it is, I think, with the
some of the paradigmatic moves made by Stephen Heath. A utopian
privileging of difference defines itself in a cluster of effects: in disparag-
ing the signifier, ignoring the imaginary, and relegating, reducing or
even trying to evade altogether the insistence of subjectivity.

4   Said

The words for 'Orient' and 'Occident' come from Latin words for sun rising (*oriens*) and sun setting (*occidens*). By nature orient and occident are relative to the positioning of the observer; the Japanese watch the sun rise in the east from the direction of Los Angeles.

In *Orientalism* (first published in 1978), Edward Said proposes that a huge and ancient historical regime has transformed this mobile positioning into a fixity, christening the 'Middle East' and 'Far East' in relation to an originary centre in Europe. On this basis the West claimed for itself the identity of a subject which could know the Orient as an object. The West accordingly considers itself authorised to speak for the Orient and its peoples: as epigraph to his book Said cites Marx: 'They cannot represent themselves; they must be represented.'

It is asserted that the habit of Orientalism – its discourse or style of thought – stretches from the Greeks of antiquity to the present day. Just as controversially, Said proceeds to bracket the real and so open for interrogation 'not only scholarly works but also works of literature, political tracts, journalistic texts, travel books, religious and philological studies' (1995: 23). He readily accepts there is a 'corresponding reality' for these factual texts, but is concerned rather with the 'internal consistency of Orientalism' (5).

Categorising and denigrating the Orient secures a particular notion of identity for the West: 'European culture gained in strength and identity by setting itself off against the Orient as a sort of surrogate and even underground self' (3). If Westerners are to identify themselves as 'rational, peaceful, liberal, logical, capable of holding real values, without natural suspicion' (Said's list), what he terms 'Arab-Orientals' are disparaged as 'none of these things' (49).

The book is a polemic: what may strike us now as deficiencies gave it edge as a strategic intervention. In 1978 it was a book waiting to be written, but today it is still hard to imagine it being done better with the theoretical resources it opts for. Said shares with Raymond Williams the distinction of founding a new discipline; if *Culture and Society* led to cultural studies, *Orientalism* made postcolonial theory possible and promoted the introduction of multiculturalism into cultural studies.

I was born in Portsmouth in 1939 (not a good choice of place or date) and grew up with the crest of the City on every lamp-post, a star surmounting a crescent moon. I noticed it but didn't think anyting about it. In fact, the emblem comes from the Royal Charter granted to Portsmouth by King Richard when adverse winds kept him in port before going off to the Crusades. I learned from Said to read it as an instance of Orientalism.

A discourse of knowledge

How far does Said avoid some of the problems that followed in the transition from Marxism to difference? Heath's analysis of narrative space was also written when Marxism was beginning to slide and is also directed at a large-scale discursive organisation, the Quattrocento tradition. I shall keep this in mind as a point of comparison. What might *Orientalism* have looked like if it had followed Heath in following Lacan?

Like 'Narrative Space', *Orientalism* is also situated within a Marxist framework: the West had a 'material investment' (6) in dominating the East. Orientalist discourse has 'very close ties to the enabling socio-economic and political institutions' (6), though Said rejects the view that a Marxist theory of imperialism can be applied 'deterministically' (12). But what sense of material determination – of superstructure by base, for example – is being rejected here? Althusser is mentioned once, but his account of relative autonomy is not explored (16). Here, as so often, *Orientalism* qualifies an assertion in an ambiguous manner. Instead of Althusser, Said explicitly endorses 'Michel Foucault's notion of discourse' (3), because it enables him to stand at a distance from Marxism, while still analysing Orientalism as 'a relationship of power' (5). Foucault argues that modern knowledges as discourses, such as medicine and psychology, exercise power in the very terms that they constitute, delimit and represent the object of their study.

Said's redeployment of this conceptualisation develops in four moves:

(1)   Orientalism presupposes a separation of subject and object such that the Western subject can know the Orient from a position of radical exteriority, one assuming a difference between being and knowledge (2).

(2)   This separation entails that the knowing subject is active and the object known is passive: 'if the Orient could represent itself, it would; since it cannot, the representation does the job, for the West, and *faute de mieux*, for the poor Orient' (21).

(3)   This metalinguistic representation of the Orient is effected by means of 'generalities' (45; see also 103, 227).

(4)   Western discourse constructs the East as though it were a non-human, non-signifying object, nature, rather than as a human, signifying object which is part of culture.

Returning later to the others, I shall take (4) first, approaching it via the geography/history distinction. This might look a marginal issue in *Orientalism*, but in fact it focuses much wider problems. Said particularly holds it against Orientalism that it operates on the model of geography, on the grounds that, 'although many learned disciplines imply a position taken towards, say, *human* material (a historian deals with the human past from a special vantage point in the present), there is no real analogy for taking a fixed, more or less total geographical position towards a wide variety of social, linguistic, political, and historical realities' (50). I know better than to get into that distinction between so-called natural and human sciences, and so am impressed by the easy confidence with which Said has recourse to an idea of 'the human' in opposing these two disciplines.

It is certainly the case that Foucault in a late essay recalled that for 'twenty years' his goal had been to create a history of the different modes by which 'human beings are made subjects' (1982: 208), but he provides no sanction for an idea of 'the human'. How does Said know that what Orientalism constructed was a human object as a natural one? It can only be that, *contra* Foucault, the object of Orientalist discourse exists outside discourse and has itself determined what may or may not legitimately be said about it. This is yet another instance of the porousness of Said's bracket round the real, a problem that is now well-canvassed. He can note a 'disparity between texts and reality' (1995: 109) and go on to contradict this by affirming with Nietzsche that the 'objective discoveries' of Orientalism are 'like any truths delivered by language', namely '"a mobile army of metaphors, metonymies, and anthropomorphisms"' (203). Moreover, Robert Young points out that Said fails to solve 'the original theoretical problem of how a representation that it is claimed bears no relation to its putative object could nevertheless be put in the service of the control and domination of that object' (1990: 130).

Appropriation

Said criticises Orientalism because it makes an epistemological separation between subject and object (objection 1 above), construes subject as active and object as passive (objection 2), and makes general statements about the Orient (3), so speaking for it and its people. (One wonders, incidentally, how well this accusation would have stuck if notions of voice and presence were replaced, as they could be, with a Derridean account of writing.) A counter to Said's disapproval here is that these three features he singles out (subject/object separation, active/passive opposition, generalisation) characterise discourses of knowledge in the human sciences in general – as, indeed, they characterise his own critique of Orientalism, for Orientalism is seen from a point of exteriority, and treated as passive, in that the object generalised about does not know what the knowing subject knows (Said, Said's readers).

As for the fourth aspect, appropriation, it is not an exaggeration to say that the human sciences are now fraught with anxiety about speaking for the other, mainly because of Foucault but in part because of Said's own dazzling intervention of 1978. Anthropology is racked over the question of how it can justify its study of (er!) 'primitive peoples'; sociology confronts a similar objection in its approach to subjects in society, but has largely managed to go on as before, living with its own bad faith; history-writing, increasingly beset by 'the metahistory question', is unsure how it can go on narrativising about people from the past as a strange tribe viewed from outside and exoticised for our amusement (Said makes a passing reference to Hayden White, see 95). In the human sciences everyone is worried about the very act of *interpretation*.

'The mere presence of a spectator, then, is a violation', writes Derrida (1976: 113), as a consequence of his discussion of Lévi-Strauss and the Nambikwara. Perhaps this whole section of *Grammatology* is too well known to require detailed citation. Lévi-Strauss romanticises and sentimentalises his experience of living among the Nambikwara; even in the unpromising situation of sleeping on earth in the open air, he feels he has direct access to something permanent and eternal in human nature: 'one of the most moving and authentic manifestations of human tenderness', Derrida quotes him as commenting (1976: 117). Derrida argues that such appropriation (not his word) inheres in the very systematicity of language, which must represent singularities as universals (generality, then is inevitable), and that all attempts at a metalinguistic perspective, by which someone, including an author, is discussed by another, compound this effect.

Lévi-Strauss looks at the Nambikwara; Derrida looks at Lévi-Strauss; the reader of Derrida's book looks at Derrida. And, you gentle reader, if you are attending to this present text, are looking at me looking at Derrida's reader looking at Derrida looking at Lévi-Strauss looking at the Nambikwara in a train of what linguists call 'embedding'. No matter how far the series is extended, subject is always separated from object, rendered external to it. A punctuality attributed to the last position can never be fully undermined, but nor can termination fully substantiate its closure.

Acknowledging that such violation is irreducible does not cut against Derrida's commitment to science. Even if the necessary structure of language epitomised in writing ensures appropriation, Derrida nevertheless affirms that 'writing is the "necessary condition" of science, that there is no science without writing' (130). For him the impasse constitutes a productive aporia which imposes the necessity of decision and action (how and why we violate etc.).

Not for Said in *Orientalism*. He nags away at the 'important task' of uncovering 'alternatives' to Orientalism, 'how one can study other cultures and people from a libertarian, or a non-repressive and nonmanipulative, perspective' (1995: 24). 'How does one *represent* other cultures?' (325).

Said and Marx

These questions and anxieties don't disturb Foucault too much, so why are they so pressing for *Orientalism*? Because it supposes a transcendental domain inhabited by a worldless subject who is in a position to resolve them. Said is explicitly devoted to humanism. *Orientalism* is offered as a 'humanistic study' of politics and culture

(15); it envisages 'direct encounters with the human' (93); believes in 'human community' (328). Recording that the book had been attacked for its humanism, Said in the 'Afterword' added to the 1995 edition responded, 'I am glad it has!' (340).

Although some of this may seem like a small-print reading, the crux can be seen distinctly in Said's intriguing discussion of Marx (see 153–5), whom he admits he finds 'puzzling'. Marx both feels sickened by the cruelty of modern economic imperialism and regards it as a historical necessity, at once 'destructive' and 'regenerating'. The society it destroyed was pre-modern ('these idyllic village communities', Marx insists, 'had always been the solid foundation of Oriental despotism'); the society it introduced was that of modernity. The theory needs to be properly grasped. Through struggle the species evolves from one epoch to another: from the 'Asiatic' mode of production to 'ancient' to 'feudal' to 'capitalist'. Each mode determines the character of its epoch, but the contradictions of each compel transformation into the next.

Said holds two things against Marx. First, that he subscribes to 'large collective terms' while ignoring 'existential human identities'. The condemnation sets aside Marx's own critique of how the collective/individual opposition is *itself* characteristic of the kind of society that, for Marx, goes with capitalism. Second, Said describes the Marxist idea that Western imperialism (he specifies England in India) laid the 'material foundations' for modernity in the East as just another piece of standard Orientalising ('lifeless Asia' regenerated by the West).

No, this is not the case. In Marx's analysis, the 'first form' of production (land owned as property) only happens to be named as Asiatic; examples are given from Romania, Peru and 'the early Celts' (1973: 472–4). Marx's account of society does not assume that Asia - or anywhere determined by that mode of production – is or was 'lifeless' and could be revived. His model – for better or worse – is *not* organic but evolutionary, referring to stages in the development of a species. Said misreads the Marxist account of how far epochs constitute all that is within them and *exclude* each other. He does so because he thinks he can write from a position beyond epochs and outside the premodern/modern opposition. More humanism, therefore.

Living inside modernity makes wondering whether it is a good thing or a bad thing an impossible question (my opinion would be that modernity means both Passchendaele and penicillin). When Said condemns collectivism and prefers individual 'human identities', he reiterates modernist ideology; when he demands that Marx should extend 'human sympathy' (1995: 154) to them, he appropriates them, just as Lévi-Strauss does in romanticising the Nambikwara. Said desires to elude the alienations of modernity, alienations of which Orientalism itself is one symptom ('wouldn't it be nice if somewhere, someone . . . ?').

Humanism

Again and again in *Orientalism* Said claims the privilege of being able to understand both East and West because he straddles them both. His 'personal investment' in writing the book derives from 'my aware- ness of being an "Oriental" as a child', though his education in Palestine, Egypt and the United States was 'Western' (25). As he puts it in the 'Afterword': 'I traversed the imperial East–West divide, entered into the life of the West, and yet retained some organic connection with the place I originally came from' (336).

This avowed taking of position carries deeper implications for the whole project. One is well publicised. Said sees Orientalism stretching from Aeschylus to the present day. Aijaz Ahmad is particularly harsh in dismissing the view that Orientalism precedes modernity as not only 'un-Marxist' but 'un-Foucauldian' too (1992: 166). An attempt at recuperation is made when *Orientalism* draws a line in the late eigh- teenth century, after which the discourse acquired 'corporate institu- tion' (Said 1995: 3).

The Greeks in Aeschylus think the Persians are barbarians, and no doubt the Persians think the same of the Greeks. In one passage Said concedes that 'some of the immediate sting' is taken out of the accu- sation that Orientalism made 'every European . . . a racist, an imperi- alist, and almost totally ethnocentric' if it is recalled that 'the more advanced cultures' have rarely offered 'anything but imperialism, racism, and ethnocentrism for dealing with "other" cultures' (204). But this lonely mention of 'advanced cultures' (as I've noticed, modernity only figures once by name, 270) hardly confronts the problem of modernity and the degree to which it constituted the whole world within its own assumptions, categories, horizons.

Humanism is responsible for the aspect of *Orientalism* I can discover least sympathy for: its endless and pernicious, high-flown, self-righteous *moralising*, which always offers readers a gratifying sense of their own moral superiority as they recognise the 'truth' of the account. This is built into the vocabulary of Said's text (for example, 'gross' (11), 'corrupt', 'blind to human reality' (326)) but it is also structured down from the premise that Western discourse established the Orient as a study of geography rather than history. Its linchpin, however, is an opposition between human and non-human. Thus: 'the Orientalist reality is both anti-human and persistent' (44); 'the Islamic Orient would henceforth appear as a category denoting the Orientalists' power and not the Islamic people as human' (87); 'humanistic values' were 'all but eliminated' by Orientalism (110) – this is the climactic end of Section 1; Ernest Renan 'treats of normal human facts' as transformed into 'something peculiarly deviant' because they are 'Oriental' (141), and his 'style' is 'antihuman except in a very conditional sense', 146; if an Arab poet writes of 'his humanity', this 'disrupts' the patterns by which 'the Orient is represented' (291). *Orientalism* wonders whether one can 'divide human reality' into ' "us" (Westerners) and "they" (Orientals)' and 'survive the consequences humanly?'(45). Later I shall have more to say about this moralising. It should not have surprised Said that the book has been widely received in terms of its 'anti-Westernism' (330).

Alternatives

Even in 1978, might it have been done differently? The only solid way to answer that question in detail would be to write a counter-text. Short of that, I shall make some suggestions, starting from the degree to which *Orientalism* already puts to work a conception of subjectivity.

Identity

When Said writes that 'European culture gained in strength and identity by setting itself off against the Orient as a sort of surrogate and even underground self' (3), the notion of exactly what sort of 'surrogate' is not defined (and instead of 'underground' we might well have expected 'unconscious'). The West's relation to the Orient, as epitomised by Balfour and Cromer, is summarised by saying, 'The

Oriental is irrational, depraved (fallen), childlike, "different"; thus the European is rational, virtuous, mature, "normal"' (40; see also 49).

On Lacan's showing, a precarious sense of identity and a good image of oneself is accompanied by disavowal of that process. The whole question of what is at stake in the way 'a collective notion' comes about, identifying '"us" Europeans as against all "those" non-Europeans' (7), the mechanisms of those identifications, positions and possibilities they afford to subjects on both sides of the we/they line, is set aside. What Said says of them is derived from Fanon and Sartre (*Anti-Semite and Jew*). So it is not surprising he can remark that there was 'very little resistance on the Orient's part' (7), a view subsequently strongly controverted (and one he has tried to recuperate since with a whole chapter in *Culture and Imperialism* on 'Resistance and Opposition').

Fantasy

Orientalism does much better in calling up the mix of fantasies caught in its textual operation. In the depths of the Oriental stage stands 'a prodigious cultural repertoire', including 'the Sphinx, Cleopatra, Eden, Troy, Sodom and Gomorrah, Astarte, Isis and Osiris, Sheba, Babylon, the Genii, the Magi, Nineveh, Prester John, Mahomet, and dozens more; settings, in some cases names only, half-imagined, half-known; monsters, devils, heroes; terrors, pleasures, desires' (63). This rich, unconscious effect is not developed.

Nor is its sexualisation. Paintings of the Orient, particularly with the late eighteenth century and Romanticism – Tiepolo, Piranesi, Gothic, Delacroix – represent it in terms of 'sensuality, promise' (118), and in Flaubert the Orient suggests 'not only fecundity but sexual promise (and threat)' (188). *Orientalism* casually makes over everyone not explicitly a woman into a 'he' but rendering of the Orient as 'feminine penetrability' (206) is left there. It is remarked that the Orient as alien is linked to elements in Western society, specifically 'delinquents, the insane, women, the poor' (207).

In 1973 in *The Pleasure of the Text* Roland Barthes distinguished between the knowable pleasures of the ego and the *jouissance* glimpsed through the gaps into our mastery. For Lacan 'desire is the desire of the Other' in more than one sense, but certainly comprehending the process by which the Other instates lack *and* desire. Said responds vividly to Flaubert's memories of his Oriental travel, in particular his experience with a prostitute on whom 'the "nauseating odor" of her bedbugs mingled enchantingly with "the scent of her skin, which was dripping with sandalwood"' (187) but does not connect this doubled threat and promise back to a deeper and more extensive mechanism of desire.

Trouble ensues for *Orientalism* from its espousal of Foucault's bracketing of the real while acknowledging that factual texts derive in part from a correspondence with it. A more thorough endorsement of the psychoanalytic account of subjectivity would have circumvented that difficulty, since fantasy is at work just as much in the factual texts of philology, geography and economics as in more obviously fictional novels, poems and paintings. Nor does *Orientalism* more than briefly consider the wide impact of the regime it describes in popular culture. That would have been readily opened up for analysis by a psychoanalytic framework.

Knowledge and Desire: Foucault and Lacan

Both Foucault and Lacan concur in thinking the subject is an effect of discourse. Lacan differs in that for him it is not *only* an effect of discourse: his assertion that a signifier 'represents a subject not for another subject but for another signifier' accepts that the subject is possessed by an autonomy not independent of the signifying system (1972: 194).

Said's humanism encourages him to worry about whether a non-exploitative discourse of knowledge is possible. At one point he recognises a need 'to rethink the whole complex problem of knowledge and power', but then is prepared to leave it 'incomplete' (24). Foucault should at least have preserved him from this humanist belief that somewhere there was a utopian outside to the whole system, though reliance on Foucault imposes serious limitations on Said's scope.

Objections to the core of Foucault's project are now well canvassed and I shall refer to them schematically here. When it is said that 'power is everywhere' because it 'comes from everywhere' (Foucault 1979: 93), we should not ask why power with its sado-masochistic connotations is preferred to other libidinal possibilities. Power works on subjectivities, but these are not considered except as an effect (the same could be said about Derrida's account of the violence inherent in writing). Deliberately halting at the frontier of the unconscious, Foucault provides no answer to the question why a subject should ever want to enter the system of discourses and institutions otherwise described so well (though only from the side of those social and ideological forces).

That there is in fact subjectivity active well in excess of anything that could be termed 'an effect of discourse' is evidenced, as Slavoj Žižek argues very acutely, when the discourses and institutions through which power would seek to regulate resistance become themselves charged as expressions of desire, for example when in the rituals of sexual confession 'the power mechanism itself becomes eroticised' (1999: 254). If the Victorians covered the legs of a piano – because they were 'legs' – that dress soon becomes a fetish. A good thing too, as Žižek goes on to assert, for Foucault is stuck with a closed circuit in which power and resistance, resistance and power, generate each other. In the first volume of *The History of Sexuality* he looks for a way out in 'bodies and pleasures' (1979: 157), what he speaks of elsewhere as 'the flesh' (1980: 211), a real beyond representation.

There is a politics here. Only a notion of the subject which goes beyond any position it is called into by discourse seems to offer the possibility of reinscribing, resuturing the anchoring points of the inherited symbolic order – as Heath shows, must become a likelihood, as desire outruns the imaginary closure of narrative space in conventional cinema.

So we are entitled to speculate about what the consequences would have been if *Orientalism* had not followed Foucault in beginning from the object and the discourse of knowledge containing it, but had begun instead with the subject whose position is assigned by a form of discourse. *Orientalism* never encompasses an explicit idea of 'the Western subject', though it is implied throughout. Said prefers Foucault, because he means to write about Orientalism in terms of a relation of power. Despite benefits accruing from this move (better answers to some questions, ability to elude the fact/fiction problem), Said may have feared that a Lacanian conceptualisation would not have dealt adequately with what Said calls at one point 'a political master–slave relation' (1995: 96). The anxiety is groundless.

In the contrast between the domains of the imaginary and the symbolic the ego presides over the imaginary, lending the subject an effect of permanence in time, stability in space and unity in the face of the fragmentation borne by the image of 'the body in pieces'. The subject's ego is defined as 'that which is reflected of his form in his objects' (Lacan 1977a: 194). That idea would have done the job of showing how Orientalism attempts to fix its objects as though they were non-human, the task for which Said has unhappy recourse to an impossible distinction between geography and history on the basis of an opposition between non-human and human. Said believes that 'Psychologically, Orientalism is a form of paranoia, knowledge of another kind, say, from ordinary historical knowledge' (1995: 72). For Lacan there can be no such distinction. All forms of knowledge develop in a 'paranoiac structure'; the ego throws 'back on to the world the disorder' which goes into its constitution (1977a: 20), a dialectic of ordering and disordering from which 'ordinary historical knowledge' certainly is not exempt.

In *Seminar 11*, arising from his discussion of Descartes, Lacan enters savage criticisms of modern science. Yes, the transcendental subject supposed by the *cogito* must come about in an epistemological scenario positing a correspondingly objective world evacuated from subjectivity. But no such scenario is any longer plausible. And the greatest misrecognition of modern science, since the time of Descartes, is to assume that there can be a relation to the other which is non-subjective, exterior to desire. There would have been no obstacle to redescribing Orientalism's discourses of knowledge along the lines on which Stephen Heath invites us to think of the particular shaping of subjectivity posed by Quattrocento space.

The signifier

Edward Said began writing as a literary critic of great insight and sympathy. Yet far too much of *Orientalism* proceeds as though the formal properties of discourse were of little account, and texts are dematerialised into colourless, weightless writing. In part this follows from the epic historical sweep foreseen for Western discourse from Aeschylus, and in part from the avowed refusal to discriminate between factual and fictional discourse (so a work of grammar goes into the account on very much the same terms as a novel). But the major explanation, I suggest, is that, following Foucault, Said moves from the object of knowledge to how the discourse construes its object on the basis of an assumed transparency in language. This might be contrasted with an approach in which the discourse was read as affording a position to the subject implicated in desire and for whom the primary relation was between signifier and subject.

Economy

Theories of ideology are open to the concept of recuperation – that there is a process by which ideology concedes and then seeks to make good its concession. In *Mythologies* Barthes reports on 'Operation Margarine' in advertising, where the tastelessness of margarine is admitted as a source of momentary indignation, only for us then to be reminded of its advantages, 'What does it matter, *after all*, if margarine is just fat, when it goes further than butter, and costs less?' (1972: 42).

Psychoanalysis promises an even better model. Once the unity of identity is surrendered and the subject understood as impossible, an economic structure is variously supposed across the split between conscious and unconscious, reality principle and pleasure principle, the pleasure principle (which excites) and what acts beyond it (which conserves), libido and the pathways it is contained within. In all these respects the subject itself is a compromise formation. Even more so with the Lacanian concept of unsatisfiable desire and fantasies whose function is to mask the lack that provokes them. Thus the Oedipal belief that you might have had a perfect relationship with your mother is, Lacan thinks, a disguise for the absence of the sexual relation. An example of a corresponding textual economy might be David Lean's film *Lawrence of Arabia*, in which Lawrence breaks the ideological generality of imperialism by showing sympathy for the Palestinian cause. At one point he brings his Arab servant into the officers' bar in Cairo. But this is then undercut through juxtaposition with another stereotype, the Englishman who imagines Arab culture as a licence for homosexuality.

A sense of textual economy of give-and-take cannot appear on the agenda for *Orientalism*. Its humanism has decided the issue already in favour of a traditional account of individual agency and authors, some of whom are less Orientalist than others. Louis Massignon, for instance (1995: 264–74), is praised because he tempers his overall view with 'Christian compassion' (271).

Moralising versus pleasure

Joined to a Foucauldian sense of 'relations of power', the opposition human/inhuman inspires *Orientalism* into a relentless moral condemnation: 'Knowledge of the Orient, because generated out of strength, in a sense *creates* the Orient' (40); 'it was the West that moved upon the East, not vice versa' (73); 'the Orient was weaker than the West' (204). Assuming such a position of judgemental exteriority would be radically undermined by any concept of subjectivity involving the unconscious, which insists on the complexity and contradictoriness of our identifications, and the more so when they are under the denial so likely with righteous indignation. There are two fairly manifest sources of pleasure in the Orientalist process.

When Said notes that 'Orientalism overrode the Orient' and asks whether 'any other than a political master–slave relation' could 'produce the Orientalised Orient' (96), he does not pause to inquire further about the master–slave relation he has invoked. For psychoanalysis it is one particularly charged with sado-masochism, inviting identification with narcissism and the drive for mastery, and at the same time with the pathos of the suffering victim. Without in any way justifying the cruelty of the coloniser, recognition of the pleasures of the master implicate the commentator in what they describe. (In *Culture and Imperialism*, which in some ways aims to make good deficiencies in the earlier book, there is a section on 'The Pleasures of Imperialism' (1993: 159–96), though these turn out to be little more than the 'boyish enjoyment' of Kipling's Kim in playing games (166).)

Second, and more briefly, there are the pleasures of the other. Without adequately exploring these, Said shows he responds well to what may occasion them in his dazzling list, which begins 'the Sphinx, Cleopatra, Eden, Troy, Sodom and Gomorrah . . .' (1995: 63). Lacan makes the repeated statement that 'desire is the desire of the Other'. This means several things, but includes the assertion that, since desire cannot come from the imaginary (the ego, consciousness and the familiar), it must arise beyond them, provoked by alterity itself. When Said comments that the West associates the Orient with feelings about 'delinquents, the insane, women, the poor' (207) he points to the pleasures of the other. *Orientalism* does not pursue this opening, nor with it the implication of all subjects in their objects.

Enunciation

I have mooted a reservation that Said's book does not give enough attention to the writing in Orientalist discourse. The signifier is also ignored in the method of the text itself, as it might not be if the opposition enunciation/enounced had figured in the analysis. What kind of book is *Orientalism*?

Said, 'a member by birth' of a minority of 'Arab Christian Protestants' (1993: 45), was bilingual between Arabic and English, and was not able to recall 'what language I spoke first' (1999: 8). In principle *Orientalism* could have been written in Arabic. It would certainly have been much harder to write within that tradition because it would have been decisively original, at least according to Said's own claim that the work of Islamic or Arab scholars 'disputing the dogmas of Orientalism' has had 'no demonstrable effect' (1995: 301). In addition, it would have been a different text, for reasons he also suggests while commenting on the Arabic translation. Here technical terms such as '*discourse, simulacrum, paradigm*, or *code* were rendered from within the classical rhetoric of the Arab tradition' (339), the translator's aim being to demonstrate that the argument could be performed as well within the Arabic as the Western tradition. Unhappy with this, Said responds a little disingenuously by saying his intervention was not meant to affirm 'antithetical identities' but rather 'to be a study in critique' (339).

Orientalism is ineluctably a work of Western academic discourse. As Ahmad points out, it belongs 'to the well-known intellectual tradition of writers debunking the great monuments of their own academic discipline', and so is comparable to disparate texts by Nietzsche, Fanon, Erskine Caldwell and Kate Millett (1992: 173–4). I think we can be more precise than this, following Said's own hint. *Orientalism* conforms to the Western Enlightenment inheritance in basing itself on an opposition between dogma and truth, superstition and actuality. It is indeed a 'critique', both in thinking it can strip away false appearance to disclose the reality concealed underneath (the power relations working through the regime of Orientalist discourse), *and* in promising to explain that appearance itself (the self-deceptions of Western claims to moral superiority disguise inhumanity, violence and self-interest). Its mission of 'debunking' would be more properly referred to as demystification.

Since my own intervention, such as it is, also partakes of the

Enlightenment discourse, I should at least state a position on this. The Enlightenment does presuppose a white, male, well-to-do, educated subject as having privileged access to reason and knowledge of reality. But the blade is sharp on both sides. For it is not possible to prevent critique extending into forms of self-criticism, as is well exemplified by the way that after 1800 a rational defence of slavery in the name of civilisation was submitted to rational criticism. If pursued – which it won't be – this argument would, I guess, find its way back to the aporia Derrida dramatises as that between writing as violation and writing as the condition of science.

Orientalism leans on Foucault for analysis of a relation of power between West and East exercised through a discourse of knowledge. Its own method relies very much on the same procedures, while seeking to denigrate them. An 'impossible reconciliation' (Ahmad 1992: 164) is tacked together between Foucault and a transhistorical humanism, this supporting both an implausibly vast sweep from Plato to Nato and a lot of preaching. It is not the case that *Orientalism* privileges difference; arguably, the space occupied by humanism performs a role taken elsewhere by that effect. But it can be accused of attending only impressionistically to subjectivity in the place of both the agent and patient of Orientalist discourse. Though all these accusations can be held against the text, they contributed immensely to its rhetorical force and so its political impact at the time.

What's wrong with postmodernism?

At the same time as it claims discourse may correspond to the real, *Orientalism* proceeds to suspend reference to reality in a discourse of knowledge. Because of the book's authority, it has continued to exercise an influence, fostering in postcolonial and other forms of theory a postmodern tendency to forget the real. Robert Young is surely right that Said's refusal to say anything about actuality has the consequence that 'any obligation to address the reality of the historical conditions of colonialism can be safely discarded' (1995: 160).

By aspiring to the notion of a non-manipulative discourse of knowledge which would transcend the subject/object relation, Said's text falls into utopianism, another trait which has been reproduced elsewhere. And *Orientalism* has also led to a regrettable prevalence of moralistic cant in postcolonial discussion. It would follow from the earlier remarks on morality and pleasure that this kind of ethical stance must veil the covert derivation of satisfaction from the other and its images – eroticism, exoticism and so on – quite apart from the position moralising offers for you to enjoy feeling right.

In this context it may be apposite to conclude with some comment on Robert Young's position in *White Mythologies* (since then his inflection has changed) because it connects with my anxiety about difference. Young is one of the most brilliant of the younger critics of postcolonial theory. However, his concluding response to Said (1990: 139–40) relies on a deconstructive pairing of unity and difference. The Orient is asserted to operate 'as both a poison and cure for Europe' because the 'kind of integral totality' Western culture imagines for itself contains at the same time 'its own impending dissolution'. Thus an 'internal dislocation' within the wished-for unity of Europe is 'misrepresented as an external dualism between East and West'. And a similar process acts between Orientalism and Said's text: the 'internal divisions' effaced in one re-emerge in the 'contradictions' of the other.

What, one may ask, enacts and energises this process? Writing itself? It's said that the West 'fantasises' its integrity, and theories get 'projected' onto stereotypes. Fantasy, displacement and projection are familiar as mechanisms of the unconscious, though Young gives no explanation of the subjective process he invokes.

5   Bhabha

Orientalism and resistance

One of the loose ends left trailing by Said in *Orientalism* was the resistance of the colonised to Western domination. This is a little strange, since Foucault particularly stresses that power is always exerted over a subject, and so always provokes resistance. Said helps to put *Orientalism* in this position by not formally opening up the question of the subject. A number of commentators have mentioned the absence of resistance, but by far the most decisive and complete intervention to make good this deficit was Homi Bhabha's.

'There is always . . . the suggestion that colonial power and discourse is possessed entirely by the coloniser', Bhabha states (1983: 200) in an early essay not reprinted in his collection of 1994, *The Location of Culture*. To put this right, Bhabha has proposed that the effort of Orientalising must always fail, since the colonial subject is constructed in 'a repertoire of conflictual positions', which render him or her 'the site of both fixity and fantasy' (204) in a process which cannot but be uneven, divided, incomplete, and therefore potentially resistant.

Bhabha has gone on to discuss a number of mechanisms which threaten colonial domination, including fetishism, paranoia, sly civility, paranoia. Though this has drawn Robert Young's criticism of Bhabha for 'restless seriality' (1990: 147), by introducing subjectivity where Said evades it except incidentally, the conceptualisation renders a necessary political service to the theory of Orientalism and to postcolonial theory in a more general sense.

What Bhabha proposes, however, is not without its own problems. These can perhaps be focused by some questions. Is the resistance Bhabha detects in colonialist discourse a sign of the active resistance of the colonised? Or is the ambivalence in fact an effect which could be detected in any text, but has been tracked down in the colonialist text by Bhabha himself? Some anxieties of this kind engage Young himself (1990: 149–52) and specifically that Bhabha's account may leave 'the problem of agency' up in the air (149).

'Mimicry'

An appropriate example would be his analysis in 'Of Mimicry and Man: The Ambivalence of Colonial Discourse', revised for *The Location of Culture*. Bhabha's use of the term is clarified in the essay by the example, developed from Macaulay and others, of an Indian man, educated in English, who works for an Englishman in the colonial civil service. He has learned colonial discourse and reproduces it; but, as Bhabha suggests, this reproduction cuts two ways, for in the act of submitting to the authority of the imposed discourse and copying it, mimicry also reveals it precisely as a construction. As Derrida might say, by demanding repetition of its conventions, colonialism requires its subjects to display the same, which, as repetition, is also, necessarily, a show of difference. According to Bhabha,

> the discourse of mimicry is constructed around an *ambivalence*; in order to be effective, mimicry must continually produce its slippage, its excess, its difference. The authority of that mode of colonial discourse that I have called mimicry is therefore stricken by an indeterminacy: mimicry emerges as the representation of a difference that is itself a process of disavowal. Mimicry is, thus, the sign of a double articulation; a complex strategy of reform, regulation, and discipline, which 'appropriates' the Other as it visualises power. Mimicry is also the sign of the inappropriate, however, a difference or recalcitrance which coheres the dominant strategic function of colonial power, intensifies surveillance, and poses an immanent threat to both 'normalised' knowledges and disciplinary powers.
>
> (Bhabha 1994: 86)

The analysis is far from straightforward. Empirically, in an actual situation, one can ask what are the motives of the participants in mimicry, master and servant. If the master thinks the servant is paying him the tribute of honest imitation, he will correct his mistakes, so corroborating his own mastery; if he decides the servant is guilty of deliberate parody, he will punish him. In what historical scene is mimicry being deployed as a political strategy (if it is)?

Bhabha's account stands well back from such issues, preferring instead an idealised notion of the free circulation of difference: 'stricken by an indeterminacy', mimicry 'emerges as the representation of a difference' and 'is the sign of a double articulation' (at once confirming and unsettling, that is). *Where* does mimicry 'emerge as' something, and if it 'is' the sign of a double articulation, is that because it just is that kind of discourse? What appears to get mislaid in here is a distinction between (to put it crudely) history and texts. This is one of those big issues (see Easthope 1999: 135–52) and all I want to claim here is that, while history is indeed a text, it is not *just* a text. Bhabha's aim is to generalise the process of simulation and dissimulation 'history' indicates, so that the term will refer indiscriminately to social and historical situations *and* to texts which may be given relatively greater meaning by a present act of reading, and where indeed the circulation of difference between text and reader may be more indeterminate.

Hybridity

Eschewing fixity and identity, Bhabha's theorisation aspires, one suspects, to a world in which difference takes over. If so, this provokes a misgiving that Bhabha's project founds itself as an adversarial discourse, that it comes about by playing off ambivalence of various kinds against a presupposed fixity, including a fixity rightly ascribed to Said's conceptualisation. The 'Introduction' to *The Location of Culture* claims there is a space 'in-between the designations of identity' and that 'this interstitial passage between fixed identifications opens up the possibility of a cultural hybridity that entertains difference without an assumed or imposed hierarchy' (1994: 4).

Hybridity generally can have three meanings, in terms of biology, ethnicity and culture. In its etymology it meant the offspring of a tame sow and a wild boar, *hybrida*, and this genetic component provides a first meaning. It is still assumed that two members of a species count as members of the same species if they can produce offspring together, while the product of a union between an Alsatian and a spaniel is a mongrel, an example of hybridity on the scientific but treacherous ground of genetics. Apart from its dire political applications, this line of analysis runs into severe difficulty over the problem of definition, a difficulty massively increased once DNA is taken into account.

A second definition of hybridity might be understood to refer to an individual 'having access to two or more ethnic identities'. This would work quite well for a literary figure such as Jonathan Swift. His avowed sympathies are High Church Tory but his texts are far too unsettling to give comfort to someone with the opinions of a Margaret Thatcher. You could say that the content of his statements, his enounced, tends to be English, while the practice of the writing, the enunciation, keeps pulling him back into a more Irish identity. It would be useful to approach Swift as an ethnic hybrid.

This limited definition would not put an end to the queries here. Does hybridity in an ethnic definition suppose that the two ethnic identities joined together were formerly pure in themselves? In any case, what is ethnicity? Like 'race', 'ethnicity' has no agreed definition. As Hutchinson and Smith say in the 'Introduction' to their Oxford reader on ethnicity, 'The meaning of the term is . . . uncertain' (1996: 4). Would hybridity in this usage also specify someone like myself, who had an English father and an Irish mother, who lived in Kerry as a child but was brought up in London? Or someone born into a working-class background who went on to university, acquiring two cultural identities? Alan Sinfield remarks, 'it is quite hard to envisage a culture that is not hybrid' (1998: 27). At this point the concept of hybridity begins to lose definition, for who or what is not hybrid? And if everything's hybrid, the term would cancel all the way through: we wouldn't need it at all.

Homi Bhabha develops his notion of hybridity from Mikhail Bakhtin, who uses it to discriminate texts with a 'single voice' (lyrical poems) from those with a 'double voice' (such as novels, whose narrator cites characters speaking in their own voice: these texts are hybridic). As with his critique of Said, Bhabha's account of hybridity can be understood as an adversarial definition; that is, it is very clear what hybridity is defined *against*, what is not hybridic.

The non-hybridic has two related features. One is a commitment to 'unitary' or 'originary' identity, identity as 'presence', identity, therefore, represented by the supposedly transcendental ego. Well set out by Descartes, this notion of the subject presupposes that thinking is to be equated with being and that its very essence is an undivided, self-controlling self-consciousness: what Bhabha refers to as 'the "individual"' that is the basis of the 'universalist aspiration' of 'civil society' (1994: 10).

Second, Bhabha believes this Cartesian concept of subjectivity is at the very centre of a Western, Eurocentric definition of culture, and a necessary support for it. One might be tempted to think of this Eurocentrism as white and male, but Bhabha avoids the risk of essentialism attaching to such terms, though only at the usual price. As Ania Loomba points out, the colonial subject in Bhabha's work 'is in fact curiously universal and homogeneous. . . . He is internally split and agonistic, but undifferentiated by gender, class or location' (1998: 179). Instead, *The Location of Culture* takes the bypass along which Kristeva theorises gender and is followed in the same lane by Toril Moi. In each case, it is the enemy who claims essence, unity and singleness of identity, so everything that may be mobilised against such an idea of unity counts as radical. An intervention, Bhabha argues, is progressive if it 'challenges our sense of the historical identity of culture as a homogenising, unifying force, authenticated by the originary Past, kept alive in the national tradition of the People' (1994: 37).

In the work of Jacques Derrida, difference undermines the sense of presence. Whenever an effect of presence is produced, it is possible to relativise and unsettle it by referring to the difference on which it rests; whenever there is anything like a coherent meaning, it is possible to point up the linguistic and discursive strategies on which such meaning depends. Difference can subvert any supposed homogeneity of meaning, truth, certainty, coherence, whatever.

Leaning on his reading of Derrida, Bhabha affirms that 'the colonial presence is always ambivalent, split between its appearance as original and authoritative and its articulation as repetition and difference' (1994: 107). Bhabha's hybridity applies a notion of Derridean difference to colonial/postcolonial texts. The presence of a dominant meaning in a dominant culture can be put in question by referring to the hybridity or difference from which it emerges.

For Derrida meaning is differential, and the difference depends on spacing, the gaps between signifiers which distinguish one from another, so that each retains a trace not of presence, fullness, but of the differentiating identity of what it is not. Bhabha's term 'interstice', borrowed from Levinas, means to respond to Derrida's account of difference as spatial differentiation. What articulates cultural differences is defined as 'in-between' spaces (1994: 1, 2, 38), 'interstices' in which 'domains of difference' may 'overlap' (2), an 'interstitial passage between fixed identifications' (4) ('fixed' here is a significant qualification).

Since difference instigates the subversion of every realm, this leaves nothing immune to the possibility of subversion. If you wanted to, you could show that what the essays in *The Location of Culture* affirm depends upon what they leave marginalised and unspoken, gaps and fissures, the graphematic feature instanced by writing. If a text makes sense, it can be undone.

So one has to ask in what sense difference specifies colonialist texts. The substitution of 'hybridity' for 'difference' aims to reassure us that we are solidly on the ground of race, ethnicity and colonial identity, but if the form of Bhabha's argument is ubiquitous, what special purchase does it have on the particular content of colonialism? On this Bhabha is a long way from Said, whose analysis of colonialism at every point indicates a historically specific content.

Other difficulties from Bhabha's invocation of Derrida carry over into *The Location of Culture*. The book refuses a notion of subjectivity which would explain, substantiate and make sense of the identity hybridity undermines. It is asserted that 'the colonial presence is always ambivalent, split between its appearance as original and authoritative and its articulation as repetition and difference' (107). Such an account does not discriminate between relative identity and absolute identity, between a coherence needed for anyone who becomes a speaking subject and a coherence which *in addition* affirms itself as its own origin, the Cartesian or transcendental ego. That distinction is made when Jacques Lacan, in the first essay of the English *Ecrits*, describes how a human being must try to achieve a stability as a speaking subject not possible for other species, and then in the second essay, on aggressivity, attacks the 'narcissistic tyranny' in which 'the promotion of the ego today culminates' (1977a: 27).

If your theorisation lacks an adequate account of presence, does this matter? It matters because failure to relativise identity means you are stuck with a notion of absolute identity, as opposed to difference, or hybridity, or the interstitial. You are therefore likely to be driven back onto a binary opposition: either full identity or no identity at all, only difference. One's hesitation then would be that privileging difference over identity has the ironic effect of treating hybridity as a transcendental signified. Instead of deconstruction, this would remain no more than an act of inversion, which stays within the original framework deconstruction undoes.

Bhabha certainly privileges difference by inviting us to try to live in difference, in a state of pure hybridity, actually in the 'interstices'. The question of community should be posed 'from the interstitial perspective' (1994: 3); to be in a ' "beyond" ' is 'to inhabit an intervening space' (7). I do not find myself drawn to accept this invitation, because what is being recommended is really only too like the state of psychosis. One way to describe the sad old man muttering to himself on a street corner would be to say he has fallen into the gaps coherent identity would conceal, and inhabits an 'interstitial passage between fixed identifications'. As Rod Edmond says, 'For many people the position of "in-between" is life-threatening, and their fragmented identities are the sign of damage rather than of discursive possibility' (1995: 39).

Texts and hybridity

It would tend to substantiate the view that Bhabha's proposals work best for purely textual analysis that the impact of *The Location of Culture* has been registered mainly in literary criticism. A consequence of its version of hybridity is to make life easy for critics of all ages. Since every text consists of an order of signifiers in a sliding and uneven relation with the meanings they open onto, since every effect of presence aimed for arises from the effacement of difference, every text can be shown to be hybridic. Any subversive pressure arising from such textual hybridity does not come from the empowerment of groups the text seeks to dominate, but rather demonstrates the skills of a well-versed Derridean reader. As Benita Parry points out, in Bhabha's own readings, 'the interlocution within the "in-between" he has construed, is a conversation scripted by the critic' (1994: 17).

Two further difficulties ensue. First, since texts can only be approached on the basis of an opposition between presence (unitary and originary) and difference, in principle no discrimination can be made between (1) those texts which seek to promote presence as a position for the transcendental ego (say, *Middlemarch* by George Eliot), and (2) those which, though establishing a degree of coherence for the subject, accept that it can never be more than temporary (say, *To the Lighthouse* by Virginia Woolf). Second, the argument blocks analysis of the textual conditions of existence of the very *different* forms of imaginary coherence texts contrive. In default of the imaginary/symbolic distinction, it is not possible for Bhabha to discriminate between the ego as absolute and as relative, and therefore between the different positions different textual imaginaries might accord to the reader.

Politics

Bhabha's adherence to the presence/difference opposition is redefined as an opposition between the Cartesian subject and hybridity; and the Cartesian notion of the individual is taken as necessary support for the 'universalist aspiration' of 'civil society' as embodied in the nation-state. Bhabha's point of view risks prejudging the nation-state and in a way that forecloses debate over its political possibilities. For example, David Miller has recently advanced a strong and detailed argument that in the conditions of modernity, nation represents the most positive drive towards democracy actually on offer (see 1995).

For *The Location of Culture* the nation-state and any form of state politics cannot be approached except as making a claim to presence (origin, homogeneity), which must be unsettled in favour of difference. This valuably compels us to attend to cultural hybridity in the form of marginalised and subordinated ethnic groupings, but at the price of evacuating the centre (the protracted battle for the franchise, forms of elected government and parliamentary politics, the whole struggle since 1789 for the rights of man and woman – a struggle which had incalculable importance in the process of decolonisation, from Ghandi to Mandela). It's hard to see how this evacuation can do more than leave a space for the reaffirmation of a unified sense of (would-be) homogeneous national identity which is anti-hybridic.

One of the most decisive of recent political events in Britain was the miners' strike of 1984–5. Bhabha gives a nuanced endorsement of the miners because they pit 'the working man' against 'the new Thatcherite city gent' (1994: 27). But his concern is with 'the necessity of heterogeneity', and so he moves rapidly to concentrate on ways that wives of miners, first seen as helpers, had achieved a new empowerment through their part in the fight. Do we have to choose between centre and margins as arenas for struggle? The political lesson I (and others) in Britain drew from the long years of Tory government, 1979–97, was the determining priority of national politics (it was of course the Conservative government at Westminster that engineered the miners' strike in the first place). No ultra-leftist 'politics of heterogeneity' based in a 'privileging of difference' can substitute for the possession of state power.

Utopia

The call to demonstrate the (inescapable) hybridity in a piece of writing and thus to 'transform the present into an expanded and ex-centric site of experience' (4) coincides with one of the more pervasive fantasies of our time: that reading texts otherwise changes the world. The work of T. S. Eliot and Ezra Pound, Picasso and Duchamp, enacting hybridity as an unanticipated interface between discourses or meanings conventionally separated, has come to be celebrated in a contemporary criticism prepared to read anything 'against the grain' if it can turn a 'text of pleasure' into a 'text of bliss'.

The wish to refuse 'fixed identifications' so we may entertain difference without an 'assumed or imposed hierarchy' repeats a desire not uncommon in poststructuralist theory and outside. That any such privileging of difference is utopian is manifest if we recall that the subject is impossible. Its imaginary identity can only be achieved at the expense of an alterity which always represents a threat to that stability: 'I identify myself in language but only by losing myself in it like an object' (Lacan 1977a: 86). It is not an option either to have a Cartesian ego on the one hand, or to inhabit the interstices between identities on the other. And was there less hierarchy in the world before Descartes than there is now?

A final word. Last summer I was lucky enough to be able to afford a week in Sorrento in Italy. Since it became fashionable, there are villas there (notably one owned by Benedetto Croce) that are worth millions of dollars. Sorrento is on a cliff, but at the bottom of the stairs to the left there is some sand and a small, impoverished fishing village. There's no lift: you have to carry the fish up by hand. No doubt, if you can believe that 'difference' and 'hybridity' constitute a more or less vacuous universality – they are constituted by hybridity as much as we are, in one big human family – you could find voyeuristic pleasure in the hard work, the sometimes riotous and spontaneous behaviour and tawdry clothes of the fishermen and their partners, as a picturesque version of the other (which would also be how they would see you). Or maybe you might respond by thinking there were other more socially specific differences arising from exploitation, poverty, bad housing and low wages. Since I cannot escape my own positioning within the Western imaginary, visiting the village from the security of my hotel, I enjoyed the spectacle. But I also didn't enjoy it.

6   Rose

In 1982 Jacqueline Rose translated essays by Jacques Lacan, collected under the title *Feminine Sexuality*, and then went on into important areas across psychoanalysis and feminist theory. However, in 1991 she made a more directly political intervention when she published *The Haunting of Sylvia Plath*. Issued by Virago, a well-known feminist press, the book was reviewed widely and favourably.

Even though Rose recognises that 'the pull' of Plath's story, especially for a particular strand in feminism, is that it calls up with such force 'a language of victimisation and blame' (1991: 6), Rose crosses this treacherous terrain with the proclamation that her own focus 'is on writing' (xi), not 'Plath herself but her representations' (2). Because of the evident significance of 'the circulation of fantasy' in Plath's texts (xii), she is also determined to exploit the resources of a feminist use of psychoanalysis in analysing Plath's writing. But approaching via the concept of the unconscious, Rose's own path means to steer clear of two dangers. On the one hand, a frequent pathologisation of Plath and her life; on the other, a feminist counter-affirmation that Plath is 'innocent' since 'man and patriarchy are to blame' (3). For Rose both these accounts are reductive, in that 'psychic life is stripped of its own logic' (3). But in following this argument into Plath's writing, she will refuse a conventional vision of Plath's poetry 'as the expression of a transcendent selfhood' (8).

The genre of poetry instances its own specificity and analytic problems related to that. A base-line definition of poetry would be that it is writing demarcated as lines, whose determining characteristic, whether in metre or free verse, must be some version of a repetition of the phonetic. This both signals and enacts the fact that poetry accords greater importance to the signifier than other modes of writing. Whatever is said about poetry must find a justification in a specific and detailed awareness of its formal particularity.

In the concluding chapter of *The Haunting of Sylvia Plath*, Rose gives just such a reading of Plath's poem, 'Daddy'. This is one of Plath's best-known texts, a longish short poem treating of her relation with her father, and a test case in discussion of her work, because it raises sharply the issue of Plath as victim or innocent. I do not intend to cite it in full (those not familiar with it will find it in Plath's *Collected Poems* (1981: 222–4)). Rereading Plath is not the point. My anxiety is whether Rose has been able to carry the entirely admirable programme she promises through the defiles of the signifier, or has been obstructed by a conventional privileging of meaning, one that would impair a reading of poetry. Inevitably, the devil lies in the detail, so, one poet, one poem. (Those who cannot engage with poetry should feel free to skip this section.)

Eliot and the 'objective correlative'

A necessary preliminary. Rose makes an issue of Eliot's concept of the 'objective correlative', so this needs a word. Emotion in art, says Eliot, can only be expressed by finding an objective correlative, 'a set of objects, a situation, a chain of events which shall be the formula of that *particular* emotion' (1951: 145). But not all poetry offers itself to be read like that. What, for example, about these lines from Eliot's own *Waste Land*?

> Who are those hooded hordes swarming
> Over endless plains, stumbling in cracked earth . . . ?
> (ll. 368–9)

Don't they invite reading in relation to social and political events in the First World War, with the 'hooded hordes' connoting use of gas-masks and 'cracked earth' trench warfare? Thus, what would incline reading in one direction or another is the *structure* of poetic representation. If the poem represents a consistent speaker, images or objects function as objective correlatives for personal emotion; if they are presented as no more than textual, part of a poem, they will attract historical meaning. (*The Waste Land* itself, I would submit, wavers between the options and excites both readings at once.)

Not so, typically, with Yeats. When 'The Wild Swans at Coole' speaks of how the swans 'All suddenly mount' and scatter 'in great broken rings', it does refer to the behaviour of swans. Mainly, however, the poem constitutes an objective correlative for emotion, a feeling for transcendent beauty and phallic power. A reader is pushed towards that because the poem so manifestly represents a speaker reflecting on what the swans mean for him.

The degree to which we read lines as an objective correlative or not turns on the poem's enunciation. If an 'I' is held together around a recognisable psychological state, a reader is encouraged to overlook the text's enunciation (along with their own positioning as its subject) and identify with the speaker represented in the poem. This gives the effect Foucault describes when he defines confession as 'a ritual of discourse in which the speaking subject is also the subject of the statement' (1979: 61). The implication of these comments will become clearer shortly.

The signifier in 'Daddy'

Jacqueline Rose's extended commentary on Plath's 'Daddy' gives most space to possible meanings of the text, arguing that it is a poem 'of the murder of the father' (1991: 222) whose narrative moves 'from victimisation to revenge' (223), a murder in which, according to the logic of the unconscious mechanism of deferred action (*Nachträglichkeit*), 'the father who is killed is already dead' (224).

The poem has been attacked by a number of critics for trivialising the Holocaust, a criticism epitomised in one view that 'Whatever her father did to her it cannot be what the Germans did to the Jews' (cited Rose, 206). Rose summarises this point of view as follows: (1) 'in aesthetic terms, what Plath is being criticised for is a lack of "objective correlative"'; (2) 'only those who directly experienced the Holocaust have the right to speak of it' (206).

In defending Plath, Rose mounts a long and serious argument against (2), asserting the necessity, even at the price of some forms of sado-masochistic identification, that those who have not directly experienced the Holocaust should encounter it in fantasy as, among other things, a means to begin to work it through in the psycho-analytic sense (this argument came alive again over the film *Schindler's List* directed by Steven Spielberg, 1993). Accepting this depends on the not uncontroversial – and certainly not in accord with the beliefs of either Freud or Lacan – view that there is a 'cultural unconscious' (8).

As for the first argument, the difficulty may be not so much the poem's *lack* of an objective correlative, but rather that it uses the Holocaust mainly *as* an objective correlative. As Rose rightly concludes, this depends on the 'conditions of representation' (214) operating in the text, a formal question. Here she advances three related assertions:

(1) The poem presents 'a crisis of language and identity' (228) caused by a process in which 'identity and language lose themselves in the place of the father whose absence gives him unlimited powers' (227–8).

(2) This crisis of language and identity is registered in the text in two instances especially. On the lines

> Ich, ich, ich, ich
> I could hardly speak . . .

Rose comments that 'The notorious difficulty of the first-person pronoun in relation to identity – its status as shifter, the division or splitting of the subject which it both carries and denies – is merely compounded by its repetition here' (226). Noting that 'In the poem, the "I" moves backwards and forwards between German and English', she refers this to 'the dispersal of identity in language' (226).

(3) Rose argues that it is the 'crisis of representation in the place of the father which is presented by Plath as engendering – forcing, even – her identification with the Jew' (227); that identification equates the father with a Nazi, so leading to images of the Holocaust, such that, as Rose says, 'Plath's poem enters into one of the key phantasmic scenarios of Nazism itself' (232).

None of these arguments quite carries conviction. Yes, the 'place of the father' – or more precisely the name of the Father – entails a crisis in language and identity, but this is a poem *about* a father. Yes, the 'I' as shifter does both carry and deny a splitting of the subject and this could be compounded by repetition. But where it carries or denies, whether it compounds the splitting or compounds its denial, depends on the context of enunciation in the poem. And code-shifting, moving between languages, is not in itself enough to disperse identity. In any case, movement between German and English is explained by the state of mind of the represented speaker who reflects upon it: 'I thought every German was you.' As for the 'phantasmic scenarios of

Nazism', I'm not myself very sure what these might be. Everyone has phantasies, Nazis included, but it's hard to see how political and ideological meaning *itself* can be in the unconscious.

Surely what is so striking about Plath's 'Daddy' is the sustained coherence of its represented speaker? A single 'I' is maintained across and confirmed at every instance, in

> I have lived . . .
> I have had to kill you . . .
> I used to pray . . .
> I never could tell . . .
> I never could talk . . .
> I could hardly speak . . .
> I thought every German . . .
> I began to talk like . . .
> I think I may . . .
> I may be . . .
> I have always . . .
> I was ten . . .

and so on to the end, 'I'm through'. No doubt, insistent affirmation of self-identity denies its own confidence; it always does. In 'Daddy' the identity of the poem's speaker is substantiated by a unified state of mind which is very much as Rose defines: in imagining her father's death, the represented speaker moves from victimisation to revenge. For an example of a radical crisis in identity and language we might turn to the closing 11 lines of *The Waste Land*.

Identity is always in play. If there is any momentary disturbance through the repetition of 'Ich', it is immediately made good when the speaker comments retrospectively on it: 'I could hardly speak . . .'. As far back as Wordsworth's *Tintern Abbey* we find representation in a poem of a speaker experiencing their own identity as in process. Far from producing a crisis that reminds us we are reading a poem, the effect is in fact to stage the speaker's state of mind more convincingly. For if you can still say 'I think I'm having a crisis', your subjectivity is still very much in place.

The speaker imagines her father as a Nazi and herself as his Jewish victim. From Romanticism on, the poetic tradition has represented speakers who refer to themselves and their own thoughts; in this way a split between subject of enunciation and subject of enounced is *depicted* by the poem as something the speaker feels, and represented *within* the poem's own enounced. According to the same strategy, represented speakers often imagine identities for themselves. The speaker of Wordsworth's *The Prelude* identifies with a version of his earlier self, just as the speaker in 'The Wild Swans at Coole' rather imagines himself as a swan. Such manoeuvres actually tend to strengthen identity by admitting and holding in place what might threaten to dissolve its stability. So it is very much in accord with tradition that the speaker represented in 'Daddy' begins to imagine an identity for herself. When she makes the situation clear, 'I think I may well be a Jew', the first 'I' is firmly in place holding up the second as a provisional and temporary identity.

A temporary identity for what purpose? Here we may retrieve the earlier discussion of the 'objective correlative'. How far is the very powerful material in the poem circulating around the fantasies Rose describes made available for contextualisation in historical and social discourses, how far as personal expression? The deciding factor is mode of representation. A condition for the contextualisation Rose claims for the text as 'historical reference' (216) would be the relatively unanchored textuality of the lines about 'hooded hordes' in *The Waste Land*. 'Daddy' does not work like this; it seeks to contain textuality so as to represent a speaker and her state of mind. The images from the Holocaust do function as objective correlatives for a personal emotion. So there is justice in the contention that 'Whatever her father did to her it cannot be what the Germans did to the Jews', if the comment means something like, 'To adapt some of the most intense and overwhelming historical events of the twentieth century as means to express mental suffering caused to an individual by a personal relationship is to diminish and reduce those events.'

Rose accepts that in 'Daddy' there is a 'preliminary privileging of the personal' (223). This privileging is not merely preliminary, however, but comprehensive, ensuing as it does from the poem's unwillingness to challenge the inherited lyric-confessional mode in which it is written. 'Daddy' is a humanist poem, and a pretty old-fashioned one, inviting comparison with work in the confessional voice of Plath's mentor, Robert Lowell, 'The Quaker Graveyard in Nantucket', and so on. Not only Lowell, but a whole tradition in English poetry stretching back from Edward Thomas through Hardy into the Romanticism of the nineteenth century, exactly the inheritance so violently disrupted by modernism. Dada and Surrealism, Eliot and

Pound, show up for us in our retrospective reading just what is the problem in such poetry, which aims to put at the centre of writing a dramatisation of the unified self. For it is poetry which seeks to express transcendent selfhood, and this is inscribed deep within the order of the signifier, shaping everything else the poem does.

7   Haraway

Our knowledge of reality cannot be absolute in the sense of being unconditioned by our positioning in time and space. Since, as Martin Heidegger says, there cannot be 'a worldless subject' (1962: 144), we can only produce knowledge within our own horizons, horizons already determined for us by our culture and a historical contingency which we both inherit and project into the future. So knowledge is discursively constructed, but it does not follow that it is therefore not knowledge. And there may well be a difference between knowledge of non-signifying objects (the 'natural world') and signifying objects ('people'). 'Natural' objects do not initiate meanings, while to understand people you to have begin by interpreting the meanings they produce.

In Donna Haraway's *Simians, Cyborgs, and Women* (1991) the essay which has attracted most attention, 'A Cyborg Manifesto', is sandwiched between others principally concerned with primatology and biology (one, for instance reviewing understandings of the langur, a leaf-eating monkey (81–108), another tracing the transformations in biology from a science centred on the organism to one of reproducing genetic assemblages (43–68)). Haraway's proposal that social and political values improperly pervade would-be 'objective' science rests largely on her work in relation to primates (monkeys rather than bishops, that is). She persuasively sustains her thesis that the scientific objectivity of primatology is compromised by human values, that we 'polish an animal mirror to look for ourselves' (21). A difficulty here, however, must be that the higher primates could well be a marginal case between non-signifying and signifying objects of knowledge; they certainly have more complex and flexible 'societies' than any other mammal beside ourselves. Primatology, more than physics or chemistry, is liable to reflect the interpreter.

According to *Simians, Cyborgs, and Women*, we are currently dominated by a philosophy of science which presupposes a 'rupture between subject and object' in order to contrast 'firm scientific objectivity and mere personal subjectivity' (8). On this basis science has tried to justify its domination of nature, a burden which has weighed particularly heavily on women. For women 'know very well that knowledge from the natural sciences has been used in the interests of our domination and not our liberation' (8). Haraway aims to break down the subject/object disjunction, undermine the attitude towards nature supporting this disjunction, and liberate women from the consequent domination. With this in mind, she turns to 'Marxist humanism' because it assumes that the fundamental position of 'the human being in the world' is a 'dialectical relation with the surrounding world' (10), such that needs create values.

Philosophy of science

In a sense we've been here before, with Edward Said's attack on how the Occidental subject appropriates the Oriental subject by seeing it from an exterior position as an object. But Haraway makes a new move when she refers to Marxism for the principle of a non-exploitative subject/object relation.

Marx, having broadly learned it and adapted it from Hegel, does indeed apply a notion of dialectic to the relation between production and consumption: 'production thus not only creates an object for the subject, but also a subject for the object' (1973: 92). However, the *method* of political economy, as he defines it, though having a roughly comparable structure of reciprocity between thinker and object of thought, nevertheless works in its own specific, knowledge-producing relation between subject and object; or rather, between abstractions already given (labour, money) and the critical transformation of them, 'a product of thinking', which is subjective (100–2). Full details here are not so important. Haraway does not develop her advocacy of the Marxist model of production/consumption; she does not follow the notion of dialectic back to Hegel (where problems may ensue from it, for instance, if it implies its own transcendence); nor does she explore Marx's own well-known statement regarding epistemology in the so-called 'Introduction' to the *Grundrisse*.

Perhaps now there are few who would dispute Haraway's general assertion that, in science as elsewhere in the human construction of knowledge, 'facts are theory-laden; theories are value-laden; values

are history-laden' (1991: 77). In fact, it would be only a slight exaggeration to suggest that many of the major thinkers from the West in this
century have circled around just these issues. My own allusions to
them will be very cursory. Heidegger, notably, in *Being and Time* (first
published in 1927), savages Descartes and the epistemology he anticipates by marking off the objective world against a purified subjectivity. For Heidegger *Dasein* is contingent in the present into which it
was thrown and from which it must project itself forward.
Understanding begins from a situatedness occurring *prior* to any
supposed opposition between subject and object.

Writing more from within the mainstream of the philosophy of
science, Karl Popper acknowledges science as at least a collective
subjective enterprise, when he declares that 'science and scientific
objectivity do not (and cannot) result from the attempts of an individual scientist to be "objective", but from the co-operation of many
scientists' (cited Quinton 1980: 32). More radically than this – and in
many ways, more accessibly – Thomas Kuhn in *The Structure of
Scientific Revolutions*, first published in 1962, asserts that all scientific
knowledge is constructed within 'paradigms'. For a while the scientific community sails along quite happily with a consensus about
methods and ends. But as new evidence accumulates of problems
with these, the paradigm on which they relied falls into doubt; this is
followed by a crisis, leading to the emergence of a new paradigm.
Kuhn has no doubt that scientific knowledge refers to reality, but
equally he makes a very strong case for the dependence of that scientific referentiality on a humanly constructed paradigm (see 1970).

In this context it is hard not to mention Rorty's *Philosophy and the
Mirror of Nature* (1980), with its sustained critique of precisely the
idea that scientific objectivity corresponds to or reflects like a mirror a
reality supposedly pre-given in nature. And on the wackier reaches of
the twentieth century's polemic around scientific objectivity there is
Paul Feyerabend. He points out that 'experience, taken by itself, is
mute' (1981: 37). For example, if Newton's theory of colours claims to
have a foundation in experiment, Feyerabend is prepared to say this
step requires two identifications, the first involving a description
which '*uses the terms of the theory under review*' (43), and the second
an equation between phenomena and experience.

To extend this list would be even more tedious than it is already,
and I have offered little more than an indication of the range of
debate. Surely this is where the action is for the issue of subject and

object in science, science as construction, the impossibility of radically separating fact and value, even on the ground of so-called 'hard' science? Yet none of these figures is discussed in *Simians, Cyborgs, and Women* or listed in its bibliography. (The Marxist philosopher, Althusser, and his contrast between ideology and science, is seen off with a quick back of the hand (1991: 186)).

A wavy line of argument, discussion, counter-argument about the constructedness of science, much tending to *support* the position Haraway avows, is dismissed as 'philosophical verbiage about epistemology' (184). One could reply that all those I've mentioned, from Heidegger to Feyerabend, are men. This would provoke questions of its own. Is patriarchy a system to be identified with men as agents, whether individual or collective? If the arguments of Kuhn, Rorty and the others are indeed compromised to any degree by patriarchal assumptions – as they may well be – surely it would be a politically progressive intervention to expose in detail how and where this leads to their arguments tending to become invalid? Otherwise, and as it is, *Simians, Cyborgs, and Women* is unlikely to make much of a dent in what it opposes. The price Haraway may have to pay for trying to bypass the prevailing conversation is that she will influence only those who already agree with her case. Isn't this strategy itself a bit utopian?

Uncertainties

Haraway does ask questions about feminism and natural science, particularly whether 'a feminist epistemology' would constitute 'a family member to existing theories of representation and realism', or whether accepting a dialectic between knowing subject and object of knowledge would effect a mode of 'non-invasive knowing' (71). The query is the same as Said's when he asked how one might study other cultures and people from a 'nonmanipulative perspective' (1995: 24). Convinced that 'subject and object can cohabit without the master–slave domination' (1991: 80), Haraway knows what she wants – an account of the historical contingency of 'all knowledge claims' and '*simultaneously*' (italics original) 'a no-nonsense commitment to faithful accounts of a "real" world' (187). She is reticent about explaining how this may be achieved.

What would happen to the principles of science supposed to govern the relation between object and subject of knowledge, if these were submitted to a feminist epistemology? Can there really be any such 'principles' (Paul Hirst for one denies that there are 'general criteria of adequacy or truth' outside specific scientific discourses, see 1979: 21.) Presumably the same problem would cover the methods of science. It is clear that the practices of science can and should work with a feminist agenda (it was once general practice in medicine to test new treatments only on men, so that they would not show variations thought to be due to women's menstrual cycle). In any case, Haraway affirms vigorously and explicitly that nothing she says should be taken as 'one more excuse for not learning any post-Newtonian physics' (186).

'A Cyborg Manifesto'

Written to explore 'a political direction' in the 1980s, the 'Cyborg Manifesto' forms a different kind of writing from that in the rest of Haraway's book, and as 'serious play', 'blasphemy', (149), maybe should not be pressed too hard. Developing from the unravelling of 1970s Marxism and a straightforward realisation that the supersession of class conflict would not itself bring patriarchy to an end, the 'Manifesto' is a self-proclaimed act of utopian myth-making, with venerable ancestors in Thomas Pynchon's figure V, the female automaton in Lang's 'Metropolis', and even Henry Adams. Utopianism is signalled in a style which treats what will be or may be as what is (so, it is said without apology, 'we are cyborgs', 150). Arising at the interface between human intelligence and intelligent electronic machines, the image of the cyborg is directed against a range of dualisms – human/animal, organism/machine, physical/non-physical, mind/body, public/private, nature/culture, men/women, primitive/civilised (163).

The list is no more unfamiliar than the movement of unsettling binary opposites, which, one might guess, enacts a deconstruction. Yet it is a deconstruction *avant la lettre* since, though *Of Grammatology* appears in the bibliography, the 'Manifesto' contributes no discussion of Derrida. Haraway's cyborg is a 'hybrid' (149, 178), and, like Homi Bhabha, she draws strength from this possibility to attack the hierarchies held to promote dualism. Like Bhabha also, she risks posing an opposition of her own between either a fixed and absolute hierarchy or hierarchies undone so far that they preclude any stability at all, not even of the most fugitive kind.

In the cyborg world, there is presumably only construction and no reproduction. There is no sexual difference – or at least it is 'a world without gender' (150), which has seen an 'erosion of gender itself' (though there are, in the same sentence, still 'women-headed house-holds', 167). Not surprisingly, therefore, it would seem there is no unconscious. It is said that 'the most promising monsters' in cyborg worlds 'are embodied in non-oedipal narratives with a different logic of repression' (150). Would this be an authentically different logic, or a logic such that there is no repression at all? The latter, I suspect.

Cyborgs – cyborgs anyway such as those in *Robocop*, *Blade Runner* and *Terminator 2* – are supposed to have no feelings, and are attractive partly to the degree that they fulfil a wish to be free from desire. They are certainly uncastrated as far as the 'Manifesto' is concerned: 'their fathers, after all, are inessential' (151). All right, no fathers, but does this mean no law either, no interruption at all of the mother/infant dyad? That's a utopia more than one person has wished for ('my mother and I were more than happy', says Hitchcock's Norman Bates). Significantly, as Fred Botting notices, the replicants in *Blade Runner* do exhibit that ineradicable trace of the mother, a navel (1999: 9).

No sexual difference, no unconscious, no lack and no identity in the imaginary. Contrary to her own determination to elude the opposition between culture and nature, Haraway praises a sense of identity marked out as 'self-consciously constructed space' as against 'natural identification' (156), and in similar terms it is remarked that for a feminist Marxist 'consciousness is an achievement, not a natural fact' (159). To ascribe identity to consciousness, indeed self-consciousness, in contrast to 'natural identification' or 'natural fact', is somewhat unclear, unless it means to discard unconscious identity as no more than an effect of the body. What is promised by the cyborg is 'affinity, not identity' (155), an idea developed with sympathetic reference to Chela Sandoval, who seeks to construct 'a kind of postmodernist identity out of otherness, difference, and specificity' (155). Apart from consciously named allegiances (affinities?), one may ask whether identity can be so constructed? Does the notion not come very close to offering us either identity given once and for all, or the end of all identity?

Two minor points on the ego as affinity or conscious allegiance.

Doesn't Haraway contradict her own celebration of the cyborg's deconstructive powers by calling on an opposition between 'consciousness' and 'natural fact'? And whatever the stated position on the dissolution of identity, the enunciation of the 'Manifesto' itself steers well clear of the wilder reaches of West Coast excess in maintaining overall an imaginary coherence and clarity.

When Haraway agrees with Hilary Klein that both Marxism and psychoanalysis depend on the view that unity is originary and 'difference must be produced' out of it, then proposes that the cyborg 'skips the step of original unity' (151), it would seem certain that this fantasy of the cyborg is able to privilege difference. Not perhaps full-blown postmodernist differance with an 'a' (Derrida 1973) (Haraway sometimes takes an explicit position against that), but a notion of difference nevertheless. Cyborgs 'are floating signifiers' (Haraway 1991: 153), free from any imaginary effect coupling them to signified meaning.

'Fusion with computers', as Claudia Springer has noted, 'can provide an illusory sense of personal wholeness reminiscent of the Lacanian Imaginary' (cited Marsden 1996: 8). This fantasy is enjoyed with some consistency. The uncastrated, father-free cyborgs preside, of course, over 'a polymorphous' information system (Haraway, 161) in which home, work, market, the body become dispersed in 'polymorphous' ways (163). And they partake of 'modern machinery' which turns out to be an 'irreverent upstart god, mocking the Father's ubiquity' (153). Defining 'upstart' as 'one that has risen suddenly', *Webster's Collegiate* uncovers the cyborg as the maternal phallus, being rather than having. Becoming a cyborg seems to imply identificaton with that.

Technology and social relations

What might make all this come about, other than as present fantasy? The 'Manifesto' gives two answers. One is that it is already there, in the imagination, in writing and especially feminist science fiction. The other is through the '"homework economy"', the new decentralising communications technologies that can put a computer in every middle- and upper-income study, so integrating 'factory, home, and market' (166). Post-Marxist is not postliberal, and Haraway retains enough of an older agenda to greet her own propositions with endearing scepticism. Contemporary and future rearrangements dependent on 'the social relations of science and technology' evoke 'strong ambivalence', though it is not necessary to be 'ultimately depressed' by them (172). This sounds a refreshingly anti-dystopian note and may be more suggestive than it appears.

Marx distinguished between the 'forces of production' (which include, for example, technology and the factory system) and the 'social relations of production', which refer to ownership and control of production. Generally, and particularly according to the Leninist hermeneutic, he has been interpreted to recommend that we should make our own history through a conscious political programme. So-called 'technological determinism' is condemned (a spinning-jenny is a spinning-jenny; only capitalism turns it into an instrument of oppression). But there is plenty of text to support a contrary reading in terms of productive-force determinism. We might better expect socialism when people form spontaneously coagulating groups, not because they choose it but because they *must* to make a living.

One more word. In political terms the cyborg myth is meant to be 'potentially helpful' for women (174). The trouble with this view is that anything – anything at all – could be helpful like this and there's just no arguing with it. On the other hand, to add some scepticism of my own, it would be very brave to claim that progressive political benefits can only come from positions backed up by good arguments.

8   Braidotti

Rosi Braidotti's collection of essays, *Nomadic Subjects*, subtitled 'Embodiment and Sexual Difference in Contemporary Feminist Theory', opens with a retrospective introduction, 'By Way of Nomadism', surveying and summarising the position developed by the whole (1994: 1–39). Other essays in the book concern pornography, monsters ('the bodily incarnation of difference', 78), Deleuze (a major influence on Braidotti), Irigaray, the European Community and other topics. Surprisingly, one of these, 'Ethics Revisited: Women and/in Philosophy', makes no reference at all to Derrida (elsewhere there is an allusion to 'the Derrida fad', 155).

Formed out of and after the thought of an 'intellectual left that has been historically defeated' (29), Braidotti commits herself to unabashed utopianism. 'By Way of Nomadism' advances itself as another myth or 'figuration', its rhetoric continually edging towards rhapsodic parataxis: political fictions 'may be more effective' than 'theoretical systems' (4). There is theory, nevertheless, though deliberately off-set with the testimony of her personal experience. In a later essay Braidotti states a need to dismantle 'the idea of reason as a set of God-given principles', while defending 'rationality' (107). It would be hard to disagree with that project, though one might want to know more about when and how exactly reason was such a set of principles – and indeed how any such dismantling (as distinct from simple evasion) might be undertaken.

Braidotti's utopian nomadism is the child of Haraway's cyborg and Deleuze (who wrote favourably about 'nomadic thought' as early as 1973). My reading of 'By Way of Nomadism' will note some of the same hesitations as I formulated regarding the utopian cyborg. However, Braidotti's refiguration of the nomad as 'a cyborg, but equipped with an unconscious' (36) will introduce additional special problems. As for the allegiance to Deleuze, a likely – in fact, obvious – query about this would be how such a radical commitment to 'becoming' can envisage any kind of imaginary stability for the *I*.

The subject

Braidotti's intervention depends on a dedicatedly anti-humanist and anti-Cartesian conception of the subject: '*cogito ergo sum* is the obsession of the west, its downfall, its folly', '*desidero ergo sum*' being a more accurate depiction of 'the process of making meaning' (13). While welcoming this admirable – many would say obligatory – starting-point, one might be put on alert by the definition of nomadic subjectivity as constituted by difference, 'in so far as axes of differentiation such as class, race, ethnicity, gender, age, and others intersect and interact with each other' (4). Is the nomadic subject an effect mainly of these or only of these? We shall see. My interest will be to track the account offered not just of difference but also of the possibility of the ego and imaginary coherence.

Not just/but also: at several points 'By Way of Nomadism' subscribes to phrasing in the hazardous form of an either/or. When there is censure of 'metaphysically fixed, steady identities', 'authentic identities of *any* kind' (5), or again, 'the illusory stability of fixed identities' (15), as with Homi Bhabha's use of 'fixed', there is a likelihood that a contrast will firm up into an opposition. And I suspect it does when Braidotti refers enthusiastically to the alternatives – 'fluid boundaries' (6), together with a not unfamiliar list of equivalents ('interstices' (6), 'in-between spaces' (7), 'heterogeneity' (17)). That suspicion becomes strengthened in such unequivocal binary oppositions as 'metropolitan space versus nomadic trajectories' (27); or the demand that feminists and other critical intellectuals cultivate a 'nomadic consciousness' and 'a sense of identity that rests not on fixity but on contingency' (31).

The unconscious

Unlike the cyborg, the nomadic subject has an unconscious, for it is subject to desire, which is 'not only unconscious', but remains 'at the very heart of our thought' (14). Desire, identification, the body in pieces and the symbolic are terms within an avowedly Lacanian vocabulary informing a stated view such as this: that the subject is 'a heap of fragmented parts held together by the symbolic glue that is the attachment to, or identification with, the phallogocentric symbolic' (12). Braidotti goes on:

> I am struck by the violence of the gesture that binds a fractured self to
> the performative illusion of unity, mastery, self-transparence. I am
> amazed by the terrifying stupidity of that illusion of unity, and by its
> incomprehensible force.   (12)

And later: 'the nomad's identity is an inventory of traces' (14).

I don't know that the body in pieces is really a 'heap', or whether
the symbolic order can best be seen as 'glue' holding the subject
together. Nor is the ego's imaginary unity an 'illusion', as though
somehow we could manage as speaking subjects without the necessity of this very real *effect*. The force of the imaginary may be 'incomprehensible', but it is not beyond analysis, far from it. Even if no
reading of Lacan can claim to be orthodox, there is a reasonable
degree of consistency in his account of the relation of the imaginary
to the symbolic.

The subject is constituted through identification. In the mirror
stage, in compensation for the fear of the body in pieces, the subject
identifies itself with an image of the body as a unity, and later with a
signifier or set of signifiers in the symbolic order. Confronted with the
lack introduced by the signifier, the subject must fantasise itself as all
the things the ego is usually assumed to be. Identity, then, is not 'an
inventory' but an act of denial. Were the gaps and fissures introduced
by the symbolic order indeed 'traces', one would have to ask what
they were traces of. Rather, lack and unity are produced together; no
originary lack is experienced prior to a desire for unified identity,
since that desire provokes awareness of lack.

Around this problem of identity Braidotti's rhetoric is particularly
fascinating. In making the statement that the unity of the self is an
illusion with 'incomprehensible force', her act of utterance, in the
words 'I am struck' and 'I am amazed', enacts just that force.

Denegation

Freud's concept of negation (*Verneinung*), instanced by a young
patient who said he had had a dream about a woman and then told
Freud not to say it was about his mother, is translated into French as
'négation' or 'dénégation'. There, going further than the notion of
denial, it has gained a more positive and active connotation (see, for
example, Derrida 1992a). Denegation works through disjunction

between the planes of enounced and enunciation, as when an explicitly stated position is undercut by what is said or enacted in the body of a text. Whether as trope or symptom, denegation has a structuring function in the rhetoric of 'By Way of Nomadism', especially in two respects.

The declared stance of Braidotti's argument is anti-humanist. Yet an origin and guarantee of its theoretical position is persistently claimed from personal experience. When Braidotti avers, 'I have grounded the depiction of the nomadic state in my own life experiences' (1994: 6), this is not a casual reference. First-person pronouns recur throughout which intend much more than any conventional usage meaning 'the writer of this text'. Along with confident gestures towards, for example, 'places where I have been' (17), there is also that peculiarly Cartesian figure correlative to the assumption that 'I know that I'm thinking' (like '*I see myself seeing myself*'– see Lacan 1977b: 80).

Such expressions as 'Maybe I just see myself . . .' (Braidotti 1994: 12), 'I think that many of the things I wrote . . .' (16), 'the nomadic subject as a performative image allows me to weave together different levels of my own experience' (7), lay claim to the immediacy of experience only at the cost of introducing a dangerous supplement. For if one *I* is doing the experiencing, who is this other *I* who sees, thinks, knows about this first, supposedly primary *I*? The problem is epitomised in the concluding line of the essay, which cites Kathy Acker with entire approval: 'I have my identity' (39). Is this a case of having your imaginary and being it? For this rousing affirmation of personal experience hardly stands on all fours with the notion of the nomad's identity as 'an inventory of traces' (14).

Braidotti's explicit invocation of 'voice' and 'voices' in the teeth of well-known criticisms of phonocentrism goes along with the assertion that 'the "nomadic" style' is best suited to give 'adequate representations of female experience', which cannot be fitted 'within the parameters of phallogocentric language' (75–6). Even discussing Irigaray, *Nomadic Subjects* omits any mention of Toril Moi's *Sexual/Textual Politics* (1985) and therefore steps aside from Moi's argument that any belief in something given as prior to representation, including the idea of female experience, may itself be characterised as phallogocentric.

Denegation extends to denying denial. How otherwise may one account for the assured assertion that no social relation is 'free of imaginary constructions' and that feminist practice must pay attention to 'identity as a set of identifications' (Braidotti 1994: 22), along-side a more than equal certainty of personal experience?

'By Way of Nomadism' says that fascination with empty spaces 'may even smack of radical chic' (16), but then denies that it does, just as it recognises that the 'nonchalant detachment' advocated for nomadic subjectivity is often 'the privilege of caste and whiteness' (21). 'Australian aborigines' are singled out as a model for nomadism (17), though also recognised as possible vehicles for a fantasy of 'unredeemed otherness' (25). Is it merely 'very hard' to change 'psychic or unconscious structures' by 'sheer volition' (31) or, if there is really a split between conscious volition and unconscious struc-tures, simply not possible at all? It is denied that 'being a nomad' means being unable to create 'stable' bases for identity that 'allow one to function in a community' (33) – but doesn't it? The actions of the Italian Red Brigades of the 1970s are saluted as 'war machines launched against the state' (26), yet later, running a women's studies department has been made possible by 'generous state grants' (34). How can a paragraph referring to Derrida lead on to another celebrat-ing 'the many voices of women' (37–8)?

One can be over-fastidious about detail (and it's a lot easier to spot others' motes than your own beams). Yet how should one read the instances I've picked out? Intended or not? Sly postmodern irony? Strategic subversion of a linear rationality declared more than once to be phallogocentric? Exemplifications of how a nomadic identity is always in transition? I'll move on to other modes in which the utopian difference of nomadic subjectivity is to find realisation.

Discourse, art, feminism

Braidotti asks us to consider three main expressions of the nomadic. The first is discourse ('The Nomad as Polyglot'). She narrates her own biography of being born in Italy, brought up in Australia, doing gradu-ate work in Paris. From this she has learned that there is 'no such thing as a mother tongue' (11), that being locked inside the familiarity of 'one language' (11) is a limitation. There is some truth in this. It does not, however, draw on the important distinction pointed out by Emile Benveniste according to which language governs organisation up to the level of the sentence, while the stringing together of sentences is the province of discourse (Benveniste 1971: 110).

In this respect you don't have to be multilingual to experience being a polyglot, as Braidotti recognises when she refers to Gertrude Stein and Virginia Woolf as writing in the same language but 'different Englishes' (15). My own view would be that the first attention should be given to the economy of a specific discourse in seeking to establish a particular relation between imaginary coherence and the heterogeneity of the symbolic.

The aesthetic promotes nomadic subjectivity because it enacts the destabilising effect of writing. Unlike Derrida (see particularly Derrida 1992b, 33–75), Braidotti readily embraces both high canonical and popular culture, choosing examples of the aesthetic potential for unsettling fixed identities from Laurie Anderson, the 'strange sounds, phonetic connections, vocal combinations' that feature in Dada writing (Braidotti 1994: 13, but see also 26), and the great modernists, including Joyce and Woolf.

To recruit modernism in support of the idea of the nomad is not at all a surprising tactic. But it faces the usual difficulty outlined here in the introductory discussion of Marcel Duchamp, and confirmed in Stephen Heath's treatment of Hollywood versus the avant-garde. (The same objection also cuts against Derrida's endorsement of high modernism in 1992b). However radical, disjunct and skewed a text may be, it does not passively and immediately interpellate the reader as a nomadic subjectivity, or indeed anything else. No text can circumvent negotiation with the imaginary into which the reader cannot fail to recuperate it.

A third enactment Braidotti espouses for nomadic subjectivity is feminism (1994: 21–8). Not certain versions of feminism more than others, but in a grand, imperial gesture, feminism *tout court*. There is no reason to doubt that Braidotti would show solidarity with any women engaged in struggling for fair wages or for legal rights, or with houseless women who, far from wanting to be nomadic in any literal sense, are trying to get off the streets (her remarks about real exiles and real migrants make this clear). Distinctions and differences within feminist politics (of which 'rights' feminism is just one example) are effaced by her incorporation, and this even though Braidotti herself stresses 'the importance of rejecting global statements about all women' (163).

Learning Resources
Centre

Airport lounges

Since Braidotti emphasises desire, it's fair to wonder what pleasures may be made available by her political fictions? At one point she announces, 'I do have special affection for the places of transit that go with travelling: stations and airport lounges, trams, shuttle buses and check-in areas' (18). Having finished all anxiety-creating preparations for travel, trusting ourselves to the big Other to service the engines and get the food ready, many of us have shared the buzz that comes from being committed to an airport lounge. But not for too long. Anyone who has had to spend more than, say, a hour at Zurich or O'Hare will concede that air travel is hell on wings.

So what desire is incited by this fantasy of being in transit? The question at once opens up a genealogy: the Romantic wanderer; the Second Empire *flâneuse*; the spiritual exile in modernism from Joyce to Kafka; Kerouac's *On the Road*, a visionary journey now domesticated in several hundred Hollywood road movies. From among many possible comments, here are two rather obvious ones. Since 1800, the pleasures of the symbolic nomad have increasingly called out something deep in the culture of the West. And as related words such as 'refugee' and 'asylum seeker' show only too vividly, these fantasies depend on *not* being an actual nomad, but rather a credit-card carrying subject free to imagine being a nomad. In Braidotti's own apt phrase, a state of nonchalant detachment.

What about the children?

'What we describe as our "character" is based on the memory-traces of our impressions; and, moreover, the impressions which have had the greatest effect on us – those of our earliest youth' (Freud 1976: 689): thus is set down a foundational concept for psychoanalysis (obviously, one that one could argue against). The inference I would draw is this. Travel, moving from place to place, will not necessarily leave babies and young children with bad memory-traces, but *emotional* nomadism is likely to be a different matter. Freud does not regard the mother or the father, or the 'natural' parents, or anyone else in particular, as needed to give emotional security, so long as the growing infant can rely on them (how could he, coming from a society in which so many babies were reared by wet-nurses?).

Babies don't get a mention in 'By Way of Nomadism', but nor do parents, or any other kind of kin relation, or friendship as a long-term attachment. This is not denegation so much as straightforward denial by omission. What may well count as denegation is the assertion that being a nomad 'does not mean that one cannot . . . create those necessarily stable and reassuring bases for identity that allow one to function in a community' (Braidotti 1994: 33).

Home

No children, no relations, community in doubt, and no home or even thought of home:

> As an intellectual style, nomadism consists not so much in being homeless, as in being capable of recreating your own home everywhere. (16)

> The nomad does not stand for homelessness, or compulsive displacement; it is rather a figuration for the kind of subject who has relinquished all idea, desire, or nostalgia for fixity. (22)

Here we come very near the knuckle. In what sense is a home you recreate wherever you are a home? Can any statement claiming that we have lost nostalgia for something lost – the precedent is Lyotard's assertion that 'most people have lost the nostalgia for the lost narrative' (1984: 41) – fail to be a denegation? It would not be hard to spot what is being denied, namely, traditional patriarchal attitudes.

These are some opening lines from a Dada poem cited by Hans Richter:

> *gadji beri bimba glandridi laula lonni cadori*
> *gadjama gramma berida bimbala glandri glassassa laulitalomini . . .*
> (1965: 42)

The writing of 'By Way of Nomadism' is a long way away from this. Despite advocating Dada and modernism – and give or take a few slippages – it seeks to secure a stable position for the reader's ego. And despite the avowed preference for rhetoric over theory, quite enough of an argument is given to incur agreement and disagreement.

What the figuration of nomadic subjectivity tries to do is dramatise the very structure of desire itself, which is defined only as transition. If so, there must be an imaginary, since in Lacan, at least, desire is an effect of the attempt to retrieve something of the real in the vector between the imaginary and the symbolic. Braidotti hopes to co-opt desire for a feminist politics. Yet desire for Lacan – as with libido in Freud – is, rightly or wrongly, neither masculine nor feminine.

9   Butler

Cyborgs, nomadic subjects, performance: though Judith Butler in *Gender Trouble* does aim for a retheorisation of possibilities around gender, she does not follow the mode of myth and imaginative refiguration. Far from it. Her work conforms rigorously to the philosophic tradition within critical and cultural theory. And it is only incidentally directed at the reading of aesthetic texts. However, once again the question of a 'utopianism of difference' is pertinent, as indeed, very specifically, is subjectivity. The further one goes in this attempt to track some recent arrivals in critical theory, the more the current situation looks like the moment after the toss, when members of the two teams head for their own end of the field: for psychoanalysis, against psychoanalysis.

Butler's 'performance' is J. L. Austin's notion of the performative utterance, with the humanism laundered out through Derrida's discussion of Austin (see Derrida 1982: 307–30). When, for example, Butler proposes that 'the enabling conditions for an assertion of "I" are provided by the structure of signification' (1990: 143), she takes a position very close to Wittgenstein (Austin's inspiration), when he argues that:

> An intention is embedded in its situation, in human customs and institutions. If the technique of the game of chess did not exist, I could not intend to play a game of chess. In so far as I do intend the construction of a sentence in advance, that is made possible by the fact that I can speak the language in question.   (1967: para. 337)

Intention is not the same as 'the assertion of "I"', though it presupposes it; Wittgenstein's 'make possible' is not as strong as Butler's 'enabling conditions'. Yet there is continuity as well as difference: both treat the *I* as an effect of language rather than anything else. What is exciting about Butler's intervention is to watch this almost venerable tradition being rewritten for radical political ends – to illuminate not chess-playing but how we might think about our lives.

Against the subject

Wittgenstein and Foucault do not make such surprising bed-fellows as one might expect. *Gender Trouble* denies the subject is an ontological given: Butler invokes Foucault to the effect that 'juridical systems of power *produce* the subjects they subsequently come to represent' (2). She develops Foucault's idea for feminism by drawing on his account of genealogy, together with his bracketing of the real, which exposes any claim of access to the real as an exercise of power, particularly of sexual power. A genealogical critique, Butler says,

> refuses to search for the origins of gender, the inner truth of female desire, a genuine or authentic sexual identity that repression has kept from view; rather, genealogy investigates the political stakes in designating as an *origin* and *cause* those identity categories that are in fact the *effects* of institutions, practices, discourses with multiple and diffuse points of origin.   (Butler 1990: x–xi)

This dismissal of any form of ontological given, including the subject, is reiterated when Butler claims that 'bodies cannot be said to have a signifiable existence prior to the mark of their gender', and suggests that bodies '*come into being* in and through the marks of gender' (8). This move, as Stella Sandford points out in a very shrewd critique, encourages Butler to assume that an '*epistemological* thesis' can dissolve 'the validity of *any* possible *ontological* claim' (Sandford 1999: 25), a lapse into idealism Butler aims to correct in subsequent work.

Rejecting any notion of subjectivity as inner truth leads Butler on to a fierce and justified attack on any feminist version of struggle undertaken in the name of a universal subject, 'Woman'. She quickly accumulates good arguments against this kind of humanism, including the knock-down assertion that if woman were an essence, it would not be possible for political action to seek to extend or transform her (15).

The allegiance to Foucault entails all the usual problems, which have been mentioned before (I might add that they would also trouble Wittgenstein's position on identity). If discourse could do it all, why can't we get the higher primates, even our nearest cousins, chimpanzees, to become speaking subjects? (Presumably because you need human culture *and* also the genetic hardware.) Granted that certain discourses and practices are given, what is in it for a subject to participate in them and reiterate them?

Gender Trouble is written in a style at once forceful and lucid, a pleasure to read in that respect. But I want to signal a hesitation about just this vigour. When, for example, Butler asks early on whether psychoanalysis is 'an antifoundationalist inquiry' whose tendency is to deregulate hierarchical sexual codes, 'or does it maintain an unacknowledged set of assumptions about the foundations of identity that work in favour of those very hierarchies?' (xii), I think we should pause to consider how far and in what sense this seemingly persuasive either/or is justified. Should we rule out any thought that psychoanalysis could act against assumptions about foundational identity *and* at the same time in other ways maintain foundational assumptions about identity? Is it right to impose this unflinching opposition between foundationalism and anti-foundationalism?

Dismissal of identity politics and adherence to a Foucauldian position is the launch-pad for Butler's attack on what she terms 'the heterosexual matrix'. Thus, 'the institution of a compulsory and naturalised heterosexuality requires and regulates gender as a binary relation in which the masculine term is differentiated from a feminine term, and this differentiation is accomplished through the practices of heterosexual desire' (22–3). There are a number of features in this structure: (1) compulsory heterosexuality, which (2) is hegemonic, an enforcement of power, and which operates (3) by establishing a series of binaries. Each term requires a denigrated other to support its definition (masculine/feminine, mind/body, universal/particular, unsexed/sexed, present/absent, identity/other, subject/not subject, within representation/beyond representation, master/slave). (4) The structure is founded on and given authority by the idea of the sexed subject 'as substance, as . . . a self-identical being' (18). (Butler cites Aretha Franklin's 'You make me feel like a natural woman', not missing the wobble evident in the comparison – 'like' a natural woman.)

Performance

The entrance fee for rest of the discussion is a pretty unequivocal either/or:

> No longer believable as an interior 'truth' of dispositions and identity, sex will be shown to be a performatively enacted signification (and

hence not 'to be'), one that, released from its naturalised interiority and surface, can occasion the parodic proliferation and subversive play of gendered meanings.   (33)

I'll come back to this, because if we submit to this binary opposition, most of the rest follows. If we discard the possibility of sex as inwardly determined, then we have already accepted that gender is *performance*, not a 'being' but a 'doing', that is to say, the effect of 'external' and socially determined linguistic and institutional practices. Having reached here, Butler feels entitled to ask about the progressive aspects of performance: 'Which possibilities of doing gender repeat and displace through hyperbole, dissonance, internal confusion, and proliferation the very constructs by which they are mobilised?' (31). In answer she invokes dressing up, impersonation, mockery of stereotypes, deliberate transvestism and transsexualism: 'I would suggest . . . that drag fully subverts the distinction between inner and outer psychic space' (137).

Making brief use of the confessional mode of discourse, I have to say this was a bit of a let-down for a reader coming from the feudal backwardness of English culture. As a child, I was taken (and later took my children) to pantomimes in which the Dame was played by a middle-aged man with both eye-shadow and six o'clock shadow, while Prince Charming was a young woman in tights. I was brought up on BBC television (there was only BBC) where famous comedians and compères were indubitably camp (you want names? Frankie Howerd, Larry Grayson).

On a more impersonal level, I would not be the first to wonder whether there wasn't a certain slide here, between performance as involuntary and performance as voluntary. These are problems touching both the author of performance and its reader or audience.

Butler picks up Fredric Jameson's well-known distinction between parody and pastiche. In parody the feeling exists that there is 'something *normal* compared to which what is being imitated is rather comic', while 'pastiche is blank parody, parody that has lost its humor' (cited Butler 1990: 138). Butler wants to defend performance as attacking something (and therefore as parody) but can't really do so without accepting (against her argument) that what is parodied is in some respect an original or a norm. So she defends performance as pastiche at the price of endorsing the view that pastiche may have no effect, be just 'blank', as Jameson says.

I would worry about something else here. For both parody and pastiche tend to be forms of comedy. Comedy is transgressive, but only if it also in part endorses the norms it exceeds. Arguably, because of the specific economy by which comedy releases inhibitions, it both reinforces values and undermines them at the same time. Butler's idea of performance must surely risk being taken as comic, and so upholding norms it is supposed to subvert.

If she is to sustain her own position, Butler must see off, or at least contain, any challenge from theories of the unconscious which describe the subject as an inwardly determined identity. So *Gender Trouble* takes an uncompromising position on subjectivity: either it is 'an interior "truth"', or it is 'a performatively enacted signification'. Joan Copjec complains that this assertion takes the form of a 'binary opposite', adding that

> Butler proceeds as though she believes that the deconstruction of the fiction of innate or essential sex is also, or must lead to, a rejection of the notion that there is anything constant or invariable about sexual difference, that sex is anything but a construct of historically variable discursive practices into which we may intervene.   (1994: 17)

A preliminary assertion of just how far Lacan thinks the subject is dependent upon, in fact integrated with, discourse would be his definition of a signifier as that which 'represents a subject not for another subject but for another signifier' (1972: 194). No subject, no signifier; no signifier, no subject.

Against Lacan

Two clouds up ahead. Butler engages with Lacan for a good chunk of *Gender Trouble*, as she must to get him off stage, along with what she takes to be his account of subjectivity as 'interior "truth"'. Lacan does not speak like a lawyer or a philosopher, and there are few interpretations of his teaching that are beyond dispute (actually, none that I can think of). Even so, too often I feel that Butler's copy of Lacan is not the one I've been reading, but another by an author of the same name. A second point is that this discussion of Lacan is going to have to be a bit technical and not very interesting for those who are not already fans.

Butler opens her critique of Lacan when she distinguishes between 'materialist and Lacanian . . . positions' (28). She revises her position on materialism in *Bodies that Matter* (1993), though not in a way which does much to rehabilitate Lacan (see Žižek 1999: 247–312), elaborating a notion of materialism which would step aside from the usual materialism/idealism opposition. There is more than enough to say about Butler without a further engagement with *Bodies that Matter*, but I would agree with Carrie L. Hull's criticism that Butler 'does not allow for the possibility that there may be different levels of materiality' (1997: 30), of which the unconscious might be one.

Butler fails to separate Lacan sufficiently from Freud. It is asserted, for example, that Lacan believes 'speech emerges only upon the condition of dissatisfaction' which is 'instituted through incestuous prohibition' (Butler 1990: 43). This 'dissatisfaction' is said to happen when an 'original *jouissance* is lost' and 'in its place emerges the sign', which 'seeks in what it signifies a recovery of that irrecoverable pleasure' (43). I'd want to know who experiences this 'dissatisfaction', where exactly it 'emerges', and where the 'original *jouissance*' ever was, such that a sign could emerge 'in its place'. Lacan refers to *lack*, not satisfaction/dissatisfaction, sees it as the effect of signification, not its cause, and does not think of it as a loss of a 'pleasure'. This scenario of paradise lost and regained is familiar and recognisable – as indeed are the spatial metaphors in which it is presented: it is the well-known story Freud summarises by saying, 'the finding of an object is in fact a refinding of it' (1977: 145). For all his determination to reread Freud, Lacan does not take this position at all, as I shall suggest in a minute, and his terminology is linguistic and mathematical.

Citing Luce Irigaray, Butler refers dismissively to 'the phallogocentrism of Lacan' (28). However, it might be that he is writing an analysis of patriarchy rather than a recommendation for it (he certainly thought he was). A similar blockage is demonstrated when Butler takes Lacan to task for invoking the viewpoint of 'observation'(49), when he may have in mind no more than the evidence of psychoanalysts and case histories. In both instances the problem is that Butler subscribes to a Foucauldian reduction of knowledge to power, and can therefore only discuss the discourses of Lacan and others as exercises of discursive power. Since there can thus be no question of knowledge as a relation between a subject and an object, Butler cannot even ask whether Lacan is right to think the symbolic order is indeed phallocentric in the way he describes. Maybe it is, maybe it isn't. I would agree with Jacqueline Rose that he is 'implicated in the phallocentrism he described' (Mitchell and Rose 1985: 56), but how far and how damaging this is remains in debate.

Lacan and sexuality

Lacan's account of sexuality is not unproblematic. A major question for me is whether he really pulls off the speculative and wildly ambitious enterprise of integrating a theory of sexuality with a theory of discourse, even though the *Graphe Complet* draws the vector of signification and the vector of sexuality in parallel and illustrates constant interactions between the two (see 1977a: 315), and even though he writes with great confidence about the phallus as being able to join 'the logos' with 'the advent of desire' (287). I'd have to agree with Lapsley and Westlake that Lacan gives no reason 'why women take up their assigned identities' (1988: 75). When Butler asks what is the '"essential part of femininity"' (Lacan 1977a: 290) that Lacan says the woman ('la femme') must give up in the masquerade, it's a good question. And Butler is right to note Lacan's difficulty in explaining what homosexual desire would be.

Butler does write acutely and accurately about Lacan's views on sexuality. But not always, and often her own reading becomes tricky. When it comes to Lacan's notion of sexual difference she offers an account which is damagingly misleading.

In his lecture of 1958, 'The Signification of the Phallus', Lacan suggests an analysis of how the symbolic order inscribes sexuality, that is, 'the structures that will govern the relations between the sexes' (1977a: 289). These precede the individual subject, who has no real choice but to identify with a position there, though a position no one could really take up, because the processes of identification and desire are always incomplete. Feminine and masculine positions are defined by reference to the phallus and, ventures Lacan ('Let us say . . .'), they 'will turn around a [wish] "to be" and a [wish] "to have"' (289). No one *has* it. And what is the phallus? A 'privileged signifier', privileged because symbolic castration, which is the same for both sexes, he insists (282), is what makes possible the signifier in general. What kind of 'phallogocentrism' is this?

Butler accepts with some reluctance that the subject in Lacan is radically decentred and cannot be thought of as self-identical, though she takes her time to acknowledge 'the possibility of multiple identifications' (1990: 67), which one might have expected her to reach earlier. But she insists that he poses masculine and feminine as a binary relation, so a relation which enforces *the heterosexual matrix.* I'm not at all convinced.

In Lacan, says Butler, 'sexual difference is not a simple binary . . .' (27). A complex one then? We'll see. The 'sexual positions' of 'being' the phallus and 'having' the phallus are said to be 'mutually exclusive' (44): but do being and having exclude each other *mutually* in the sense that 'a/not a' is mutually exclusive? That is what you'd expect when Butler affirms that 'in order to "be" the Phallus' (Lacan is not responsible for that capital letter) 'women must become, must "be" . . . precisely what men are not' (45). Yet if this were Lacan's view, surely he would have discriminated the two positions as either having/not having or being/not being? When Butler writes of the 'binary restriction on sexuality' (54), she may not have Lacan in mind, but she certainly does when she refers to 'the binary disjunction of "having" or "being" the Phallus', adding that the consequence is that 'the excluded term of the binary' returns to haunt it (66).

A difficulty hanging over all of this is that it's not clear what Butler means by a binary. Nevertheless, there are grounds for arguing that the two (desired) positions of having and being do not constitute a binary opposition because, though both are referred to the phallus, they are not symmetrical. If this were doubtful in the essay of 1958, it can hardly be put in question in Lacan's rethinking of the symbolic order in his diagram of sexual difference in *Seminar 20,* delivered in 1972–3 (see Mitchell and Rose 1985: 149–71), a text *Gender Trouble* does not discuss. I shall leave readers to examine this for themselves, and satisfy myself here by remarking: that the formulae for masculine on one side and feminine on the other contradict each other; that the masculine and feminine sides of the diagram are shaped as (1) a line and (2) a two-sided angle; and that there is only one possible site of masculine *jouissance* but apparently two available from the feminine side.

Two minor points. It is conceivable that empirical men and women may at different times and in different situations find themselves divided between different positions on the diagram of possibilities. From time to time Butler gives the impression that having the phallus is definitely better than being it. I'm not so sure, since having the phallus would only lend the man a signifier and, moreover, one 'which has no signified' (Mitchell and Rose 1985: 152); the phallus isn't his; he doesn't really have it; and it wouldn't be satisfying anyone's desire even if he did. Is Lacan also being phallogocentric when he refers to the man's phallic *jouissance* as 'the *jouissance* of the idiot' (Mitchell and Rose 1985: 152)?

A prelinguistic determinant

Butler argues that Lacan supports the heterosexual matrix by holding to a substantive view of sexuality as founded in a prelinguistic reality. She remarks on 'the pervasive nostalgia for the lost fullness of *jouissance* in his work' and that 'the very inaccessibility of the past . . . confirms that original fullness as the ultimate reality' (56). Now, it may be possible to read Lacan like this. He certainly accepts that there is a real for human subjects and this includes the kind of biological real Freud began with. Lacan mentions the premature birth of the human species as a factor in provoking the mirror stage, and when he refers to an 'original dereliction' in our origins (1977a: 27), I assume he's thinking of that.

But attributing a notion of original fullness to Lacan does not respond to two crucial aspects of his teaching. One is the rejection of anthropological conceptualisation in favour of linguistic and later topological thinking. This is evident when, for example, he asserts that 'the unconscious is neither primordial nor instinctual; what it knows about the elementary is no more than the elements of the signifier' (1977a: 170). Second, Lacan endorses a Heideggerian commitment to thought as possible only within the horizons within which it arises and is situated. Thus Lacan suggests it is effectively impossible for a speaking subject to have any idea what it's like to be a baby, who is *infans* ('not speaking').

There is indeed an extra-linguistic real in Lacan. But when Lacan tries to describe the relation between the real and the symbolic as that between being and meaning, it soon becomes a wry joke, because naturally the discussion can only take place on the terrain of meaning. Within being, 'the subject disappears', and it appears within meaning only on condition that 'it emerges in the field of the Other' (1977b: 211), that is, alienated within the symbolic order of shared signifiers, none of which can belong uniquely to anyone.

Being is not 'an original fullness', since it is the real, simply itself.

Being does figure within meaning, not as something retrieved, but rather as radically reconstructed within and on the grounds of meaning. Something – a trace of something, an absence, a want-to-be – is carried over in the subject from the real into the symbolic. It causes desire, though it can only be experienced in desire's effects, in the objects imagined to replace it (*Gender Trouble* omits the question of desire in Lacan).

What introduces lack into the subject is the structure of the signifiers, rendering impossible the real and the world of need. So Lacan points out that '*jouissance* is forbidden to him who speaks' (1977a: 319). Law grounds itself on this abyss between being and meaning which Lacan refers to as an 'almost natural barrier' (319) (natural in the sense that he refers to the birth of the symbol as the death of the thing). But it does so in a particular way, by retrospectively recasting this impossibility as the incest prohibition. Through this fantasy we can still imagine the mother is available (if only . . . there wasn't the incest taboo), when it is rather that for the speaking subject she is impossible. It is just not the case that for Lacan the subject is founded in 'a primary repression' associated with the 'maternal body' (Butler 1990: 45). And when he states in *Seminar 20* that 'There's no such thing as a prediscursive reality', because 'every reality is founded and defined by a discourse' (1998: 32), his meaning could hardly be more explicit.

Freud does indeed encourage the view that there is some original fullness which is lost, when he writes that 'the finding of an object is a refinding'. In underwriting this assertion, Lacan introduces a crucial difference:

> The object is by nature a refound object. That it was lost is a consequence of that – *but after the fact* [my italics]. It is thus refound without our knowing, except through the refinding, that it was ever lost. (1992: 118)

The only lost fullness here is in our own present fantasies.

It's easy to accuse others of fantasy. However, when Butler not only claims that Lacan believes in some 'original fullness as the ultimate reality' (1990: 56), but adds that Lacanian Law means that everyone's sexuality fails to retrieve what was promised or possible there, something strange is going on. Does this inevitable failure, as she says, really recall 'the tortured relationship between the God of the Old

Testament' and his would-be obedient servants (56)? Not for me, I must say, on those rare occasions when I have been deceived by the delicious misrecognition that there is a sexual relation, with the usual appurtenances, and then undeceived. Butler concedes the 'comedic dimension' of Lacan's 'failed model of reciprocity' between sexed subjects (45), but seems to have lost her sense of humour entirely when she later responds to what she calls 'the structure of religious tragedy in Lacanian theory' (56).

The heterosexual matrix

Butler's accusation is that Lacan reiterates once again the heterosexual matrix. This is defined according to several features. It presupposes 'stable', that is, substantial sexual identities (1990: 151, n. 5), such that 'masculine expresses male, feminine expresses female', a sexual relation that is defined 'oppositionally' through 'heterosexuality' (this last clarified elsewhere as a differentiation accomplished through 'the practices of heterosexual desire', 23). But in Lacan sexual identities are not stable or substantial (they depend on identification); masculine and feminine are specifically *not* expressions of male and female bodies; the positions accorded of wanting to have and wanting to be the phallus are not oppositional or, if they are, only in a vague and general sense.

It is not in dispute what heterosexuality means for Butler, as in her example from Aretha Franklin. Here's another, the closing exchange in *The Big Sleep*:

> Bacall: You've forgotten one thing – me.
> Bogart: What's the matter with you?
> Bacall: Nothing you can't fix.

So he can make good her lack just as, implicitly, she can supply him with what he lacks, warm human sympathy. Now that's what I call a heterosexual matrix. But according to Lacan it just doesn't and can't exist because – along with many other reasons – of the structuring asymmetry of available positions. In Lacan there can be no 'heterosexual desire', any more than there can be homosexual desire or masculine desire or, as Butler thinks, 'feminine desire' (47). The object of desire can never be more than an endlessly shifting object whose cause appears only in its effects; any features it has at any time (masculine, feminine or whatever) are endlessly subject to change. I would say the case against Lacan is not proven.

No subject, so utopia soon?

Gender Trouble asks its reader to choose between discourse and subjectivity, unequivocally opting for discourse. From Wittgenstein out of Austin, Butler takes the view that performance is a sufficient explanation of subjectivity, that the rules of sentence formation explain intention, that the *I* is an effect of language and only language. Perhaps this will work if discourse is considered to consist of 'words', the already completed sign, though Butler's account must be put at risk by the distinction between signifier and signified (one which does not seem to impress her).

In contrast, Lacan affirms that where you have signifiers there must be a subject and vice versa, that the subject's imaginary is stitched together with the symbolic order. For example, it follows a sentence or holds together a sequence of sentences along the syntagmatic chain. According to Lacan, as each signifier (or cluster of signifiers) arrives, we anticipate what signified meaning will emerge later on, while retrospectively pushing aside meanings that, as one says, are not relevant to the context (see 1977a: 303). At the anchoring point or *point de capiton* – often in written English signalled by a full stop – coherent meaning is held in place, temporarily, and the imaginary appears present to itself, temporarily. Yet meanings set aside are not deleted – there is, Lacan observes, always a 'sliding of the signifier under the signified' (160).

What works as an anchoring point is determined both by the structuring of the symbolic order *and* by the process of the subject. The subject is an effect of the signifier; and it acts in a related effectivity in its own process of desire. *Nec tecum, nec sine te*, neither with you nor without you, as Beckett remarks of a wished-for sexual relation.

Butler's analysis of sexuality (and, by implication, much more) as performance is utopian in the sense that it does not admit to a persistent, structuring and ineluctable alienation between the subject and the symbolic order, between desire and the Other, that there can be no fitting or happy alignment between 'self' and 'society'. For *Gender Trouble* the only obstacle to satisfaction is the prevailing order of discourse, which in principle can be reinscribed through performance to accommodate any version of desire. All we need to do is get rid of agreed structures through which 'already established identities are communicated', and then 'identities can come into being and dissolve depending on the concrete practices that constitute them' (1990: 15–16). As mentioned already, I'm sceptical about the radicalising consequences of performance thus conceived.

In *Bodies that Matter* Butler revises her view to include the possibility that performance subverts and reinforces at the same time, an argument she develops further in *Excitable Speech* (1997). How much difference does this qualification make, I wonder? Doesn't it just mean it will all take a bit longer to work through the 'already established identities'?

The necessary condition for Butler's vision of an endlessly progressive reiteration at the level of culture is that we discard an 'interior "truth" of dispositions and identity' in favour of discursive construction. This is not exterior, since there is no interior which is not its effect, a position reinforced when *Bodies that Matter* states that 'construction is neither a subject nor its act, but a process of reiteration by which both "subjects" and "acts" come to appear at all' (1993: 9). But doesn't this still leave Butler with the question of how and through what discursive effects desire, whether for a temporarily 'heterosexual' or 'homosexual' object, could ever arise?

A note on reading

I will end with a somewhat sour couple of paragraphs. Butler is not a very reliable reader of other people's texts. Having detailed examples from *Gender Trouble*, I shall add a note here on *Bodies that Matter*, specifically from the chapter attacking Lacan, 'The Lesbian Phallus and the Morphological Imaginary' (Butler 1993: 57–91). Her argument that there can be a 'lesbian phallus', since the phallus is 'fundamentally transferable' (83), assumes that the phallus is some kind of thing or entity (why otherwise should Butler think that 'having the phallus' is a 'relation of property?', 63?). This is a total misrepresentation or misreading of Lacan's notion of the phallus as effect of a structure which may afford a position to the subject. There can no more be a 'lesbian' phallus than there could be a lesbian equals sign (=) in mathematics. It is not the case that for Lacan the phallus 'originates or generates significations' (60), nor can the Lacanian real be equated with 'the maternal presence' (70).

Bodies that Matter seeks to show that, despite his frequent denials, Lacan regards the phallus as the penis because it is derived, in the mirror stage, from a bodily image that is masculine – 'a body part', says Butler, 'has been elevated/erected to the structuring and centering principle of the world' (79). To sustain this view Butler proposes that in Lacan's analysis of the mirror stage 'a lived sense of disunity' leads the child to project 'ideality and integrity' modelled on its mirror image (75). In fact, the mirror image initially perceived offers the child only a '*Gestalt*' (Lacan 1977a: 2), which in turn manufactures for the subject a 'succession of phantasies' (not perceptions) of possible disunity ('the body in pieces'), which in turn ('correlatively', 5) compels the child into identification with an imaginary counterpart. The image of the body is definitely not 'in pieces before the mirror (i.e. mirror stage) and before the law', as Butler avers (1993: 81), a case where a conditional ('If the body is "in pieces" before the mirror . . .') has become a fact by the bottom of the next page (80–81).

Butler supports her argument that Lacan's phallus is the penis by citing *Seminar 2*: 'certain organs are caught up in the narcissistic relation, in so far as it structures both the relation of the ego to the other and the constitution of the world of objects' (Lacan 1988b: 95; Butler 1993: 76–7). She concedes that the these 'organs' are 'not named' (77), but does not hesitate to enter another slippery conditional ('If these organs are the male genitals . . .', 77), which is once again taken up retrospectively as a statement. The passage in *Seminar 2* is not about organs and narcissism but a subtle technical account – a reply to a Dr Perrier, in fact – regarding psychosomatic problems. An organ is named and it is 'the eye' (Lacan 1988b: 95). The passage does not say what Butler claims it does; her readings should be taken with a pinch of salt. When she admits 'one might be tempted to argue that . . . the penis becomes the phallus' (Butler 1993: 77), the temptation is hers, not Lacan's, and one she seems unable to resist.

Butler can't leave Lacan alone and has returned again to the topic in *The Psychic Life of Power* (1997). Slavoj Žižek has given a sustained and, in my view, entirely convincing critique of her arguments there in *The Ticklish Subject* (1999: 247–312).

10 Dollimore

Critical theory instituted a continuous demand to retheorise from the ground up. In *Sexual Dissidence* (1991) Jonathan Dollimore rethinks the traditional social and religious condemnation – and often brutal persecution – of homosexuality and, particular in Dollimore's concern, male same-sex activity, as what he terms 'the perverse dynamic' (the equation between homosexuality and perversion is his). I will have to ask later what this new theorisation can do which we could not do already. For the basic effect of the perverse dynamic is already familiar as the psychoanalytic mechanism of projection and displacement. Dollimore quotes James Baldwin as saying, 'Straight cats invent faggots so they can sleep with them without becoming faggots themselves' (cited 1991: 219). Desire denied in one subject is projected onto another object, who can then be held responsible for its origin, promotion and very existence. Unconsciously, of course, this would not take place unless the straight cats were not as straight as they thought.

The perverse dynamic

Homophobia has provided a fearful instance of a larger process which Freud sardonically generalises in terms of a structural relation between God's perfect goodness and Satan's absolute evil:

> Nobody wants to be reminded how hard it is to reconcile the undeni-able existence of evil . . . with His all-powerfulness or His all-good-ness. The Devil would be the best way out as an excuse for God; in that way he would be playing the same part as an agent of economic discharge as the Jew does in the world of the Aryan ideal.
>
> (cited 1991: 128)

Naming it as 'the perverse dynamic', *Sexual Dissidence* defines a similar structuring in the relation between dominant and subordinate orders in society:

> an irruption within the dominant destabilises the binary oppositions legitimating that order. The binary is then in part restabilised through renewed control of those signified by its inferior term, who are typically identified as inverting, perverting, or deviating from the prevailing order, and in the process have displaced onto them responsibility for the disruption occurring elsewhere.   (112)

Three main influences are apparent here. A Marxist notion of dominant and subordinate classes (blocs, groups, cultures) is worked together with Derrida's deconstruction of binary oppositions and the ineluctable dissemination of difference (Derrida is explicitly signalled, 65–6). Foucault is also present in the argument that power maintains itself by constructing behaviour and attitudes as perverse.

Sexual Dissidence is a generous, lively and, if I may risk it, kind-hearted book, but it provokes interrogation nevertheless. A key issue is why it rejects an account of subjectivity as unconscious – Foucault is notoriously antagonistic to psychoanalysis – when the perverse dynamic, said to operate through perversion, deviation and displacement, appears a fundamentally unconscious mechanism. For Dollimore there is a 'theoretical tension between psychoanalysis and materialism' (170) which denies the status of materialists to Freud and Lacan. This aligns him exactly with Judith Butler's distinction between 'materialist and Lacanian . . . positions' (1990: 28). If psychoanalysis is not a theoretical materialism, what is it, I wonder? In one respect Dollimore's impatience with psychoanalysis leads him into a strange mistake, which may even be symptomatic.

One might have expected Dollimore's project to conduct him towards a detailed and specific history of the social oppression of same-sex desire. In fact, the range is far more eclectic than this, as the subtitle affirms, *Augustine to Wilde, Freud to Foucault.* There is, I think, a major problem here. Deprived of a demand for attention to the symbolic order, and dismissing regard for the specificity and autonomy of signifying practices, *Sexual Dissidence* cannot but establish the perverse dynamic as though it were a structure with some kind of transhistorical essence. Certainly, the dynamic is able to embody itself more or less in the same form in an extraordinary number of different fields and activities: metaphysics, ideology, the social formation, subjectivity (including sexuality), literary texts. In each case the signifier is treated as effectively transparent.

What exactly *is* the perverse dynamic and where does it live? Is it, as is said at one point, one of our 'structures of thought' (143)? If so, how does it operate across philosophy and the social formation and subjectivity and textuality? Is it always the same in shape and function, a process in which the opposition between dominant and subordinate, like that between thesis and antithesis, is resolved not by synthesis but rather by displacement and demonisation? Or, perversely, is the perverse dynamic always different in its specific effectivity?

Philosophy for Derrida is a particular kind of writing. His own endeavour to shake traditional loaded binary oppositions has been aimed specifically at the sort of logical oppositions which have typified Western philosophic discourse. Dollimore leans on the Derridean manoeuvre, and it is consistent with this that the perverse dynamic should be displayed most convincingly on the terrain of metaphysics.

Christianity has always faced the problem of evil Freud mentions in the passage cited above, and so risks falling into the Manichaean heresy that good and evil are coeternal and equally powerful. Augustine – in principle – rescues theology, by denying that evil has any positive force of its own, since it consists only in the privation of good. But as *Sexual Dissidence* argues, the idea of perversion is required to negotiate between evil as agency (a mode of being) and evil as pure lack (that is, non-being). Dollimore demonstrates very persuasively that, since evil as privation is implicitly defined as the lack of something which *ought* to be there, 'evil as an essential absence becomes a haunting pervasive presence' (142). So a logocentric struggle to expel difference only discovers how normal goodness was always already divided against itself.

Good and evil are conceptual moral categories, whose content is defined in advance; undoing Augustine's metaphysical oppositions, then, is very much a question of demonstrating logical incoherence. But the relation between dominant and subordinate in the social formation may not be at all the same as that between metaphysical good and evil, since the social formation is an empirical historical phenomenon. As supported by the institutions of bourgeois culture, the dominant order has been repressive and insufficiently democratic; it has scapegoated what it defines as disorder and perversion as means to justify its use of force, as well as its moral right to govern. And perversion comes from within the dominant order: law only prohibits what people do and the police are as liable to corruption as anyone. As fiction teaches, every Holmes is secret kin to Moriarty, every Clarice in love with Hannibal Lecter.

The perverse dynamic may indeed 'disclose important dimensions of both social struggle and antagonistic (social) interdependence' (122). But in another way, it may not. Although murderous aggression, racism and homophobia continue to irrupt within the dominant order, as they may within anyone, it is surely right that the democratic and progressive side of the dominant order should seek to expel them, should treat murder as a crime, restrict freedom of speech for racists and legislate the same age of consent for all forms of sexual preference. The dominant order (if that's what it is) should declare perverse murder, racism and homophobia themselves. Even if the normal procedure of law indeed embodies a version of the perverse dynamic (and it does rather sound like it), it would still be good old-fashioned anarchism to be opposed to law in general.

Subjectivity

Besides the particular mechanism of projection, the perverse dynamic might feature within the psychoanalytic account of subjectivity in two main ways. One could regard the 'dominance' of conscious over unconscious as a mode of the perverse dynamic, in that potentially destabilising effects arising within the ego (for instance) are prevented from doing so overtly if they become adequately repressed. But unlike the opposition between conflicting forces in the social formation, the relation takes the specific form of a subjective unity split by an interactive dynamic, the *Spaltung* in which conscious and unconscious come about as conditions for each other.

That topographical and dynamic relation is the condition for an economic effect on the grounds of sexuality and in terms of the choice of a sexual object, where the finding of an object is a refinding. Since what remains with me from being outside discourse drives what I now desire within discourse, every sexual object represents a deflection or deviation from an imagined original.

Sexual Dissidence claims (1) that for psychoanalysis sexual perversion is inherent and universal, and so (2) Freud's attempt to discriminate between heterosexuality and homosexuality in relation to the Oedipal transition is inconsistent: 'Perversion proves the undoing of the theory which contains it' (197).

With (1) there's no problem. Laplanche and Pontalis, in their authoritative dictionary of psychoanalysis, argue just this view, pointing out that 'it is difficult to comprehend the idea of perversion' without 'reference to a norm' (1973: 306). With (2) the situation is different. The aetiology of male homosexuality (female homosexuality follows a different path) is one of the less controversial areas in Freud's psychoanalysis. Following the polymorphous-perverse stage in infancy, the little boy emerges, like everyone, with a bisexual potential; faced in the Oedipus complex with Hobson's choice, he may either risk castration in 'active' desire for mother or equally by 'passive' identification with her. Identifying with her, he may also be drawn to 'a narcissistic object-choice' for one of his own sex. But 'behind this latter factor there lies concealed another of quite exceptional strength, or perhaps it coincides with it: the high value set upon the male organ and the inability to tolerate its absence in a love-object', this leading to aversion from women, 'even horror of them' (Freud 1979: 206). 'Probably no male human being is spared the fright of castration at the sight of a female genital', and some 'become homosexual as a consequence' (Freud 1977: 354). According to Freud, Leonardo da Vinci became homosexual because he came to see his mother as a vulture.

In *Sexual Dissidence* something curious happens at just this point in the discussion of Freud. When it reaches the aetiology of male homosexuality (1991: 196–8), *Sexual Dissidence* turns from Freud's own theorisations to accounts of writing around that explanation by Henry Abelove, then Jeffrey Weeks, followed by one C. A. Tripp, followed by Kenneth Lewes and finally John Fletcher. How can the book tolerate the absence of Freud's account of the fear of castration as cause of male homosexuality? The reading of Freud, then, is partial (Lacan hardly gets a look-in). In the absence of psychoanalysis, how does one explain what informs and energises the process of *displacement* through which the perverse dynamic is said to operate?

Textuality

Since Dollimore is not unwilling to elide a number of differences in order to isolate the perverse dynamic, it is not surprising that textual reading is treated very much as content analysis. Besides *The Tempest* (109–13), a main chapter concerns *Othello*, giving particular attention to the following lines:

> OTHELLO: And yet, how nature erring from itself –
> IAGO: Ay, there's the point: as (to be bold with you)
>   Not to affect many proposèd matches
>   Of her own clime, complexion, and degree,
>   Whereto we see in all things nature tends –
>   Foh! one may smell, in such, a will most rank,
>   Foul disproportion, thoughts unnatural.
>   (III.iii.229–35, cited 152)

Dollimore comments, 'Here Othello imagines, and Iago exploits, the paradoxical movement of the perverse: a straying *from* which is also a contradiction of; a divergence which is imagined to subvert that from *which* it departs in the instant that it *does* depart' (152). Fine, no problem, this is an acute remark on the content of the exchange. But in what sense is the perverse dynamic referred to here the same as in the other examples? For in this instance of textuality surely something different is going on?

Othello is a fictional text, not a novel but a play. We are therefore invited to read these words in a specific manner – not only for their avowed meaning (though it's certainly there) but in the context of dramatised characters and their dramatic situation at the time. In the context (surely this is not a subtle point?) a main effect has to be not the meaning, but that Othello and Iago here converse almost as equals, so that Iago can say to his master, 'to be bold with you'. Here a mutual rehearsal of the perverse dynamic becomes grounds for *collusion*. That kind of variable effect is due to the operation of the signifier at a level deeper than that of any signified content. In fictional textuality the perverse dynamic must have a force and effect different from what it has elsewhere.

Defined as 'an irruption within the dominant', which 'destabilises the binary oppositions legitimating that order', because perversion lies at order's own centre, the perverse dynamic begins to sound a bit like Bhabha's hybridity. Although what has been denounced as perversion shifts across cultures, in the Christian culture of the West it has had a relatively stable identification as buggery, sodomy, homosexuality (coming later to include female homosexuality). Problems accrue if it is generalised beyond particular historical situations in specific modes of signifying practice. Derrida's deployment of the presence/difference distinction, to which the perverse dynamic owes so much, does not suffer from this danger of abstraction, at least in his own writing: Derrida is nothing if not a respecter of what is distinctive to a form of textuality.

Shorn of its psychoanalytic roots in projection and presented as exclusively social, the perverse dynamic lacks explanatory value – a dynamic, in fact. But it has to be so shorn, because perversion is effectively impossible to define, except in social terms. Dollimore gives a good reading of Freud to the effect that a disposition to perversions 'must form a part of what passes as the normal constitution' (Freud 1977: 86). When Dollimore remarks that 'we are presumably all perverts now' (1991: 175), he is presumably right, for a liberal position today would be that the preference for having sex with people of the same sex should be treated as neither more harmful nor of greater public concern than a taste for train-spotting, an enthusiasm for meteorology or an obsession with the pastoral elegy. Dollimore would contest this. Since sexuality touches every aspect of the human experience, so he proposes, to define what counts as illegitimate sexuality is integral to the exercise of political and social power. It was, but it is now only for a decreasing minority. And if we are all perverse, a view on which Dollimore and Freud concur, then the perverse dynamic starts to leach any useful content. Like hybridity, if it is everywhere, it is nowhere in particular.

Sexual Dissidence has very little to say about why in any one of its various instances the dominant order should organise itself in the way it does, what its own conditions of possibility might be, what pleasures might attach to its effect of displacement, what its *imaginary* might be. So why the perverse dynamic? Is it not another way to privilege difference? Dollimore makes gay sex sound great fun, which is fair enough, though even if every man feels homosexual desire, full-blown unsublimated acting out may not be every man's cup of tea. In any case, as Žižek rather mischievously points out, it is no accident that those who 'like Michel Foucault, advocate the subversive potential of perversions, are sooner or later led to the denial of the Freudian

Unconscious', because the unconscious 'is that which, precisely, is *obfuscated* by the phantasmic scenarios the pervert is acting out' (1999: 247–8). On this showing, perverse activity masks unconscious desire, rather than embodying it. Is Dollimore subject to the old Romantic fantasy that perversion is a real feel which is better expressed?

1 1   Eagleton

Now for something completely different. In *Heathcliff and the Great Hunger* (1995) Terry Eagleton confronts the reader with eight essays on Irish culture and society since 1750, offering a comprehensive coverage that moves easily between history, philosophy, literary criticism, cultural theory and, occasionally, abbreviated biography, keeping a thoughtful distance from both nationalist extremism and historical revisionism. I want to discuss the book because in some significant ways it does elude the general criticism of privileging difference, while at the same time slipping into what in my argument are the common faults of denigrating the force of the signifier and giving insufficient attention to subjectivity.

Far, indeed, from fetishising diversity, *Heathcliff and the Great Hunger* can be accused of privileging identity, sameness, the imaginary. No imaginary can in fact be hermetically sealed, but Eagleton's imaginary seeks to close itself by co-opting a guarantee for itself from the real. This, however, is a real of a particular kind, a Marxist real: that is, social interests defined by class oppression. In *Ideology: an Introduction* Eagleton asks us to imagine a social location specified as 'third galley slave from the front on the starboard side', someone who has to row 'non-stop for fifteen hours', while 'sending up a feeble chant of praise to the Emperor on the hour' (1991: 206). Discourse theorists, he argues – Eagleton has in mind Hindess and Hirst (1977) – would say the slave's feeling that he would do well to escape from his chains was no more than an interpretation of his situation.

Eagleton will have none of this. After a sarcastic paragraph mocking such 'interpretations', he asserts that what the slave rightly interpreted was enforced by 'the *fact* [italics original] that this situation was oppressive' (1991: 208). And his conclusion is that 'the "real" here certainly exists prior to and independent of the slave's discourse, if by the "real" is meant that specific set of practices which provide the reason for what he says, and form the referent for it' (208).

In a review of *Ideology: an Introduction*, Richard Rorty writes that Eagleton's evocation of the galley-slave repeats a Marxist habit of assuming that pain is prior to language, while suggesting that those who do not see suffering like that are oblivious to it. Citing the paragraph leading up to the claim that the slave's oppression was a *fact*, Rorty accepts that the real exists outside discourse. However, he points out that it is one thing to say the real exists, but quite another to say that sentences about the real are true on the grounds that they accurately represent, or correspond to, the nature of the world. Rorty has no doubt that the slave would be better off if he tried the discourse of emancipation, but condemns Eagleton for seeking – despite denegations – for support from the way things intrinsically are.

In *Heathcliff and the Great Hunger*, as we shall see, on the almost unbearable question of the Famine itself, Eagleton aims to secure the book's imaginary to the extra-discursive fact of class exploitation and the nature of the capitalist system. The very consistency and steadiness with which his theory of political economy holds in a coherent perspective such a troublingly diverse range of discourses, facts, histories, lives, texts, unifies the book's material — at the price of a certain ruthlessness. Eagleton imposes a very strong reading (without it, for example, I'd never have realised that Bram Stoker's *Dracula* 'like the Ascendancy, is running out of land' (Eagleton 1995: 215)), but by the same token provokes questions about what lies outside the limits of his narrative, about the other it must necessarily deny.

The signifier

Eagleton's history starts from around 1750. Recognition of an Irish cultural inheritance from before then is set aside by the chronology, while at the same time commitment to the priority of political economy would tend to exclude it in principle. Yet traces of this great Irish oral tradition, bardic, heroic and romantic, constantly return. A main argument, and not a surprising one, is that Irish writing generally eschews realism, and Eagleton acknowledges that one factor at work is that such textuality recycles 'the riddling wordplay and extravagant dream world of the ancient sagas' (149). Part of an Irish willingness to elevate culture over politics, Eagleton says, does derive from 'the Gaelic political order', brought low in the seventeenth century

but, 'in the form of bards and ballads, music and memories', living on
as 'one of the few remaining repositories of a "national" consciousness' (234). And that structure of feeling still sustains an 'anti-mimetic
aesthetic' down as far as Wilde and Yeats (333). The objection here is
not that Eagleton does not accord weight to 'the old Gaelic order'
(185), still less that he fails to make it a *sole* determinant (whatever
that might mean); it is rather that acknowledgement of this effect
breaks into the theoretical space of *Heathcliff and the Great Hunger*
from a position officially outside, and when it does get in, it appears
undertheorised, a given.

'The slightest alteration in the relation between man [*sic*] and the
signifier . . . changes the whole course of history by modifying the
moorings that anchor his being', writes Lacan (1977a: 174), affirming
the very real material process by which a particular discursive formation produces and reproduces the subjects that in turn produce it.
Bound to the iron logic of a binary opposition between 'idealism' and
'materialism' (see 1995: 8, 63, 118, 145, 148), Eagleton remains deaf to
the siren calls of the signifier. He writes with assurance of the
thematic and narrative aspects of the Anglo-Irish novel, for example,
but rarely responds to the textuality of that writing. I find it symptomatic of this asceticism that he hardly ever quotes. Eagleton's Joyce is
more politically correct than Derrida's (see Derrida 1992b: 253–309),
but much less farouche.

Another procedure is available: to begin with an account of the
discursive formation of the national culture, asking what identifications this offered to the subject, and entering into a political assess-
ment of what the culture made it easy to say, or what it
correspondingly inhibited. This would grant more autonomy to the
signifier, as well, perhaps, as attributing more independence to
Irishness, instead of reducing history to the universal demand that
one paradigm fit all occasions. But it wouldn't have been political
economy.

Subjectivity: Ireland, the English problem

Though it might seem strange to suggest this, since it is drawn on
frequently, another exclusion from *Heathcliff and the Great Hunger* is
psychoanalysis and subjectivity. Eagleton turns confidently and
acutely to notions of Oedipal aggression, displacement and disavowal

to discuss the 'stalled dialectic of love and hate' which grips 'the Anglo-Irish mind', so that its idealisation of Westminster matches its detestation of the Irish masses (1995: 71). A well-argued passage explores the possible psychic structuring which informs the endlessly contradictory coupling between Ireland and Britain: it is a relation like that of incest (128) or of a 'tormented Lawrentian couple' (131); it embodies Adorno's account of identity foisted upon non-identity (131), or a form of 'Hegelian logic' (132) in which contradiction and non-contradiction are both feasible.

Eagleton settles for understanding the England/Ireland affair on the Lacanian model of the always incomplete dialectic between subject and subject at the level of demand:

> the other must interpret one's demand for what it is; but one can never be entirely sure that this has happened, given that the demand itself, in order to attain expression, must pass through the defiles of the duplicitous signifier. The meaning of speech depends upon the response of its addressee; but since this response, too, must pass through the ambiguous medium of signification, we can never be entirely sure that our demand has been acceded to. For another thing, the other will receive one's demand only from within the distorting perspective of his or her own desire, which will then render it doubly opaque.   (141)

Eagleton's recourse to psychoanalysis is only locally persuasive, however, because, quite simply, the unconscious is conceived as an adjunct to the process of political economy, a coincident effect. But the unconscious has its own time and cannot be limply nailed onto the prior temporality of history.

Yes, indeed, the relation between England and Ireland, like the failed intensity between lovers, was always one of misrecognition. But there are degrees of misrecognition, and Eagleton is right that exchanges between these two nations were particularly 'garbled' (139). The two national cultures pass each other like ships in the night, or better, like one tectonic plate sliding over another. Again there is a failure to attribute sufficient power to the signifier. Communication had to take place between the Lockean discourse of the English, committed to truth, fact, common sense and the transparency of discourse, and an Ireland in which, as Eagleton recognises, language is 'performative rather than constative . . . anything, in fact,

but *representational* (170–1). For grim centuries English empiricism
and the Irish rhetorical tradition swerved past each other, so that
almost any other coloniser – France, China – might have stood a
better chance of understanding Ireland than the one history came up
with.

The Famine

Ireland is the British Empire's oldest colony, and for nearly a thou-
sand years the English have been committing atrocities there that
they would never have carried out at home. There is an Irish proverb,
'Ceithre nithe nách tugtha d'Éireannach ionntaoibh leó .i. adharc
bhó, crúb chapaill, dranna madra agus gáire Sagsanaigh', which
means, 'Four things which an Irishman ought not to trust – a cow's
horn, a horse's hoof, a dog's snarl and an Englishman's laugh'.
Thomas Carlyle was hardly going beyond prevalent Victorian attitudes towards the Irish when he exclaimed, 'Black-lead them and put
them over with the niggers' (cited Hackett 1919: 227). In the years
1844–9 a million Irish starved slowly to death (about one in six of the
population), while exports of butter, eggs, meat continued to flow out
of Cork and Dublin to the English mainland.

Auschwitz, as Adorno said, introduces a crisis of representation. It
is impossible to speak of the Holocaust and impossible to keep silent.
In Derrida's version, 'the thing remains unthinkable', and 'we still
have no discourse equal to it' (1995a: 287). Part of the impossibility
lies in naming the atrocity, for a name is unique to its bearer, yet can
only appear within the universalising system of language. So, Derrida
argues, there are 'names other than that of Auschwitz and which are
just as abhorrent'(cited Lyotard 1989: 386). One of those names is the
Great Hunger of Ireland, yet to find analogies for it, to generalise
about it, to write about it at all, is to betray its complex historical
specificity.

Eagleton states that the Famine was 'the greatest social disaster of
nineteenth-century Europe – an event with something of the charac-
teristics of a low-level nuclear attack' (1995: 23). There is a 'striking
paucity' of Irish writing about the Hunger (12), as if from trauma; in
reparation Eagleton puts it ineluctably at the centre of his own book
and compels attention to the fact by his title.

Heathcliff and the Great Hunger makes three separate attempts to write about the Famine. It begins, certainly, by accepting that it was an event which continues to defy representation, 'the Irish Auschwitz' (13), threatening the 'death of the signifier' (11). In a second move Eagleton argues, against some nationalist writers, that 'there was no question of calculated genocide' (24). And then, edging his account back into line with the larger tendency of his text, he spurns what he calls 'the typical gesture of Irish historiography' – to take the property relations of nineteenth-century Ireland 'as some unquestionable context' (22) – and insists on making that context itself responsible:

> The answer is doubtless complex; but it must surely include the fact of a vastly inequitable system of agrarian capitalism which was implanted by the British, run by their political clients, and conducted largely for their economic benefit.   (25)

Ultimate responsibility belongs not with the landlords or the English, but 'with the system they sustained' (25).

The Famine sounds like genocide. Cecil Woodham-Smith records the state of Irish emigrants on some ships in their passage and arrival in North America, including the following:

> On June 27 [1847] Whyte was kept awake all night by 'moaning and raving from the hold', and cries for 'water, for God's sake, some water'. The mate, who appeared 'frightened and quite bewildered' told him that 'fearful scenes' were taking place below – the 'effluvium' rising from the hold was so overpowering that it was impossible to go on deck. A medical officer at Grosse Isle recorded that, visiting an emigrant vessel in the morning, 'I have seen a stream of foul air issuing from the hatches as dense and as palpable as seen on a foggy day from a dung heap.   (1962: 224)

The same causes of starvation and typhus meant that the British soldiers experienced the same thing when they opened the sheds at Bergen-Belsen in May 1945.

Do people *calculate* genocide – genocide as such? This raises the very troubled question of acts and intentions, hard enough to settle in individual acts (though courts of law have protocols for deciding intention), but much harder in the case of collective movements and government decisions. My view is that those who commit atrocities do not think of what they are doing as atrocious. More likely, they will feel it is their duty, even a repugnant duty, and that – however difficult to understand in hindsight – was certainly the case with the Nazi perpetrators of 'The Final Solution', who believed they were fulfilling a eugenic responsibility to culture and civilisation.

From 1844 the British government was constantly fussing over efforts to stave off famine in Ireland without spending too much money. They knew, therefore, the effects of the decisions of 1847, which cut off previous forms of relief and made the Irish poor-law system responsible for preventing death by starvation. Those administering Ireland from London carried out what they felt was their unenviable duty. (James Donnelly endorses A. J. P. Taylor's view that the main leaders of policy towards Ireland in the crucial years, Lord John Russell, Sir Charles Wood and Charles Trevelyan, 'were highly conscientious men, and their consciences never reproached them' (1993: 33)). It was, nevertheless, as the Lord Lieutenant of Ireland wrote on 26 April 1849, 'a policy of extermination' (cited Woodham-Smith 1962: 381). When Eagleton refers to 'the Irish Auschwitz', it sounds as strange as would a reference to 'the Jewish Auschwitz'. The Great Hunger was an English Auschwitz.

For Eagleton the English are exonerated from 'calculated genocide' and responsibility reassigned to the capitalist system which preceded the Hunger and made it possible. If the Hunger is caused by the system, then the real is still rational, though we are left with the question whether the same system always produces the same consequences as were inflicted on the Irish people between 1845 and 1849. If one does not find Eagleton's conclusion an adequate and substantial response, then his account of the Famine is another instance of the more general problem of reducing complexity to fit political economy and, in this instance, not sufficiently respecting difference.

12   Grossberg

Long walks

The English artist Richard Long does walks, sometimes recording them with photographs and maps. A photograph from 1967 shows 'A line made by walking'. There is also a square of pebbles positioned on a Somerset beach, a circle of stones in the Andes and an arrangement of driftwood on a beach in Alaska. Clearly this enterprise marks a relation between human activity and the natural world, recognising the priority of external nature and the relative impermanence of human intervention. But it is crucial to its meaning and effect that such work cannot be bought and sold, resisting commodification and recuperation by the world of dealers, galleries and museums: as Long says, 'Some of my stone works can be seen, but not recognised as art' (Fuchs 1980: 236). He spurns reference in favour of act and practice: 'My art is the essence of my experience, not a representation of it' (236). Long's work is almost invisible, on the very verge of impossibility. Are his constructs indeed useless experiences and not useful representations? Could they be? Well, there are the photographs, otherwise we might not know about them at all.

Cultural studies

Cultural studies was invented by Raymond Williams with his book *Culture and Society* in 1958. It is as anti-aesthetic as Richard Long's work, rejecting an approach to culture in terms of what is located in galleries and museums, and indeed, in terms of the present canon of great literature. *Culture and Society* is determined to open debate about all aspects of society's artefacts, by recontextualising them not as 'works of beauty' but as texts produced and reproduced by cultural practices. Affirming that high and popular culture should be studied together and on equal terms, the works of Shakespeare alongside Hollywood, the pop music industry and tabloid newspapers, cultural studies has attacked the domain of the institutionalised aesthetic as aggressively as Dada ever did.

It has rejected the traditional idea of a purely evaluative reading of culture for what can summarised as four reasons:

(1)   The aesthetic sanctions the art of the gentry or ruling class, even though high culture has no automatic claim to be better than the culture of ordinary people, the working class.

(2)   The aesthetic encourages formalism, an approach to texts as objects in themselves, divorced from their social, political, ideological meanings.

(3)   The aesthetic treats texts in their supposed universality, ignoring history and the historical constitution of their meaning.

(4)   The aesthetic fetishises texts as objects for consumption, disavowing the labour by which they are produced and reproduced.

Things have moved on since Raymond Williams, and especially, as we shall see, in the United States. Here is a recent example of attitudes current in cultural studies. I choose it not in a spirit of self-justification, but because it is ready to hand. In 1992 in *Literary into Cultural Studies* I proposed that the paradigm of literary study was increasingly giving ground to a new paradigm in cultural studies. The book was reviewed in 1992 in an American journal, *The Science Fiction Research Association Review*, and the argument attacked on the grounds of its conservatism.

In concluding, the critique asserted that cultural studies was committed to 'a radical eclecticism', and that this

> is not a paradigm at all but a perpetual state of crisis corroding the boundaries of traditional forms of knowledge. What it emphatically does *not* need is a coherent . . . ideology of the sort Easthope attempts to give it.   (Latham 1992: 18)

By 'coherent . . . ideology' I suppose Rob Latham means an attempted theorisation within the discipline of cultural studies. What is striking –

and, by this point in my account here, only too familiar – is the deployment of oppositions to support the assertion. On one side there is a theoretical paradigm, the boundaries of tradition, forms of knowledge, coherence; on the other, radical eclecticism, the corrosion of boundaries, perpetual crisis and something supposed to appear entirely outside rational coherence.

What is peculiar about this advocacy of crisis and flight from theory is that cultural studies, while developing rapidly, is not at present notably already in crisis, and has a respectable body of theory and consensual attitudes to draw on, at least in the British inflection.

A brief *aide-mémoire*. In the first phase, Culturalism (1958–74), Raymond Williams and Richard Hoggart redescribe culture as an attribute of the whole of society, not merely its privileged members. Humanist, empiricist and moralising, the work of Williams mounts a grim-jawed argument to validate working-class culture precisely *as* culture. At the beginning of this phase Hoggart writes against the Americanisation and embourgeoisement of traditional English working-class life, on the grounds that it leads to what he contemptuously dismisses as 'a candy floss world' (1958: 169). Aestheticism is identified with Oscar Wilde, Bloomsbury, homosexuality, and the decadent wing of the upper class.

A second phase, Marxist Structuralism (1975–85), associated particularly with the Birmingham Centre and the work of Stuart Hall, reinforced this traditional British puritanism, by drawing on both Althusserian Marxism and semiology, to offer an analysis of (mainly popular) culture in terms of relative autonomy. Fortified with the visionary certainty afforded by its commitment to science and theoretical practice, cultural theory served as a high place from which (like Moses on Mount Sinai) you could see far beneath you the toiling masses enslaved to the ruling class through their addiction to Hollywood, soap opera and pop music. Suspicious of 'art' as a form of ideology, this second phase of cultural studies shared with the first a dedicated hostility to aesthetic evaluation.

A third phase, Postmodernism, roughly since 1986, has reacted strongly against what it sees as the dogmatism and theoretical closure imposed in phase two. It rejects the Sinai view that the theorist knows best, instead explaining the pleasurable and even empowering potential in popular culture. Phase three has kept asking questions in a theoretical framework but is more pluralist in its theoretical sources – semiology, ideology, gender, ethnicity and others – without feeling a need to anchor theory in a tradition. But it has reiterated the populist, sceptical and anti-authoritarian stance which has been there since Williams.

My main example comes from an international gathering. In 1990 a massive conference, 'Cultural Studies Now and in the Future', brought 900 people to the University of Illinois at Urbana-Champaign, and later 40 of the papers were published as *Cultural Studies*, edited by Lawrence Grossberg, Cary Nelson and Paula Treichler (1992). Part of the collection's deliberate strategy was to make cultural studies hegemonic in the United States and this fostered some vagueness and would-be inclusiveness in its presentation.

In the editors' 'Introduction', which for simplicity I have ascribed here to Grossberg, cultural studies is defined in the first place as an academic outsider. It is 'anti-disciplinary' and 'has no distinct methodology' – or rather, 'no methodology can be privileged . . . with total security', while 'none can be eliminated out of hand' (1992: 2). Conversely, it is affirmed that 'cultural studies cannot be just anything' (3). What then? The nearest we get to a specific definition of cultural studies is its political concern: in the words of Tony Bennett, cited with the editors' approval, a 'commitment to examining cultural practices from the point of view of their intrication [*sic*] with, and within, relations of power' (3). Theories of cultural studies have attempted 'to connect to real social and political problems' (6). The sense of this connection is rather unpredictable: now you see it, now you don't. 'Although there is no prohibition against close textual readings in cultural studies', the 'Introduction' assures us, 'they are also not required' (2); culture consists of both 'a way of life', including 'institutions, and structures of power' (that is, susceptible to sociological analysis) *and* 'forms, texts, canons' (that is, textuality) (5).

Of course, the 'Introduction' is strategically right to seek to draw practitioners together rather than exacerbate differences, but some inescapable difficulties follow from its excitedly politicised avant-gardism, in other words, its slide into the beyond. This comes out not only in the wish to define cultural studies as outside convention (anti-disciplinary, pragmatically pluralist in methodology) but also in passages such as the following:

> cultural studies is continuously undermining canonical histories even as it reconstructs them for its own purposes. Constantly writing and rewriting its own history to make sense of itself, constructing and

reconstructing itself in response to new challenges, rearticulating itself in new situations, discarding old assumptions and appropriating new positions, cultural studies is always contextual.   (10)

The breathless syntax and cumulative participial repetitions warn us that more is at stake than merely the rational self-reflexiveness incumbent on any serious intellectual practice. Cultural studies in this account, like continuous revolution, defines itself as beyond the canon, so far beyond that it remakes 'canonical histories' for itself. On this showing, cultural studies, its practice and theory, has come to have something of the status of a Duchamp readymade or a Long walk. It attempts only too obviously to privilege its own difference from any sustained institutional activity, or any single self-critical and developing theoretical paradigm. Difference itself becomes the object of the exercise.

13 Žižek

Appparently, a group of Marxists in Slovenia in the 1970s read Althusser and, like others of that time, were directed to the materialism of Freud and Lacan. One of them, Slavoj Žižek, would probably call himself an orthodox Lacanian. We'll see. Certainly Žižek studied in Paris, is in touch with Jacques-Alain Miller and Lacanian circles there, and has spent time on all of Lacan's texts, including the eleven of 27 seminars that are available only in *samizdat* from certain bookshops in the rue des Ecoles.

Ernesto Laclau and Chantal Mouffe in *Hegemony and Socialist Strategy* (1985) condemned as imaginary misrecognition all conceptions that the social formation was a harmonious unity, and insisted that the social exists as an effort to construct an impossible object:

> Any discourse is constituted as an attempt to dominate the field of discursivity, to arrest the flow of difference, to construct a centre. We will call the privileged points of this partial fixation, nodal points. (112)

They explicitly refer these discursive points, at which the social appears to stabilise itself, to Lacan and his account of the *point de capiton* (anchoring point). Žižek comes in on the back of this take, with *The Sublime Object of Ideology* (1989).

I would count at least five Žižeks: Žižek the Lacanian; the analyst of culture (both high and popular); the philosopher; the theorist of sexuality; the Marxist. I shall concentrate here on the first two of these, Žižek the Lacanian, and how his position works in application to cultural texts. All his readings have a certain wonderful, in-your-face outrageousness. (It might be hard to better Terry Eagleton's crack when he says Žižek would argue that we go to sleep because there are beds around.) Žižek's own justification for this in *Looking Awry*, subtitled *An Introduction to Jacques Lacan through Popular Culture* (1991), is that he 'mercilessly exploits popular culture' as a 'convenient material to explain not only the vague outlines of the Lacanian theoretical edifice but sometimes also the finer details missed by the predominantly academic reception of Lacan' (vii).

Given the position I've taken myself in this text, it would seem churlish not to greet Žižek with open arms as a much-needed ally, who almost single-handedly has restored Lacan to the contemporary agenda. I do welcome his intervention, but will not be deterred from setting Žižek at a critical distance. I worry about his version of Lacan; I have reservations about its effectiveness; and I am not put at my ease by the fact that he is a little coy when it comes to citing references to Lacan's own work for some of his own key concepts. Maybe he feels he knows the seminars too well to bother, though it's undeniable that he goes too fast, as though anxious about the silence that might leap from any gaps opening in his breathless progress.

Reality and the real

Since Althusser, Slavoj Žižek has given a completely new impetus to the relation between Marxism and the unconscious in a series of stunning performances, from *The Sublime Object of Ideology* (1989) on. Whereas others have *begun* with Marxism and attempted to incorporate psychoanalysis into it, Žižek starts with subjectivity and then moves out towards the social.

For Žižek, as for Althusser, ideology is not so much what we consciously think as something we unconsciously practise – when we behave, for instance, '*as if* the President incarnates the Will of the people, *as if* the Party expresses the objective interests of the working class' (1989: 36). What Žižek terms '*ideological fantasy*' consists in overlooking 'the illusion which is structuring our real, effective relationship to reality' (32–3). Referring to Lacan's discussion of the dream, 'Father, don't you see I'm burning?', Žižek says, ' "Reality" is a fantasy-construction which enables us to mask the Real of our desire', and 'it is exactly the same with ideology' (45). The true goal of ideology is '*the consistency of the ideological attitude itself*' (84); thanks to ideology, '*pure difference is perceived as Identity*' (99); ' "Let the facts speak for themselves" is perhaps the arch-statement of ideology' (1994a: 11).

Misrecognition, identity, consistency, the self-evident: in Lacan these are all effects of the imaginary – what masks through fantasy the real and the symbolic, conferring the effect of stability on the ego. Žižek's 'ideology', like Althusser's, is essentially the Lacanian imaginary.

'The *Titanic*'

This is very suggestive. I shall test it with two of Žižek's prolific examples. In the process, the question where his project integrates Marxism and psychoanalysis will more or less answer itself:

> the sinking of the *Titanic* had a traumatic effect, it was a shock, 'the impossible happened', the unsinkable ship had sunk; but the point is that precisely as a shock, this sinking arrived at its proper time – 'the time was waiting for it': even before it actually happened, there was already a place opened, reserved for it in fantasy-space. It had such a terrific impact on 'social imaginary' [*sic*] by virtue of the fact that it was expected.   (1989: 69)

Žižek notes that a novel of 1898 even foretold such an event. Transatlantic liners were 'floating palaces, wonders of technical progress', 'the meeting-place of the cream of society' (70). What sank was a symbol of society 'as a stable totality with well-defined class distinctions', in a 'barbaric' accident which represented 'the approaching catastrophe of European civilisation itself' (70). It is not the case, then, that something happened and people responded, but that the 'social imaginary' was already in place and seized on the event.

But there is a problem here, which I think is endemic. Who is this 'fantasy-space' or 'social imaginary' present to? And who experiences the sinking of the *Titanic* as a symptom? It can only be some collective Western subject living around 1912. But that is not how desire masks itself in either Freud or Lacan, for whom the unconscious and its censorship, like the dream, are your own, not collective. No doubt the Victorian *fin de siècle* was taken up by people in all kinds of fantasies (melancholia, neurotic anxiety, the death wish, etc.). But we should not miss how Žižek runs together the operation of fantasy with a specifically *social* content, ideology in the sense of meaning shaped in relations of social power. The 'floating palaces' do figure as fantasy objects, but their meaning as a 'stable totality with well-defined class distinctions' is something else altogether. However plausible and persuasive Žižek's analysis, fantasy and social meaning, the unconscious and ideology, are *superimposed*, not unified.

A second question we would need to pose is: who resists this fantasy? For there is no question here of a partial or uneven identification. Like Althusser's interpellation, Žižek's 'social imaginary' appears to function perfectly for everyone. This theory is very interesting, but one has to ask whether it is really a theory that involves the unconscious as understood by Freud and Lacan. At this stage we should note the query and move on.

Nazi anti-Semitism

Fascism aimed to solve the problem of politics by eradicating political conflict. To do this, it sought to abolish the necessary and inescapable differences that inhere within even the most apparently unified culture. But as Slavoj Žižek proposes, in his brilliant discussion of Nazi anti-Semitism, this project of establishing 'a totally transparent and homogeneous society' (1989: 127) is condemned to impossibility in advance. The ' "Jew" is a fetish which simultaneously denies and embodies the structural impossibility of "Society": it is as if in the figure of the Jew this impossibility had acquired a positive, palpable existence – and that this is why it marks the eruption of enjoyment in the social field' (126). Such a fantasy thus contains its own attempted solution in advance, for every possible alterity and heterogeneity will be gathered together and projected onto the fantasy image of 'The Jew'. 'Society is not prevented from achieving its full identity because of Jews: it is prevented by its own antagonistic nature, by its own immanent blockage, and it "projects" this internal negativity into the figure of the "Jew" ' (127), which can then be held responsible for a blockage which is actually fundamental.

This is a valid and persuasive insight into the nature of racism and the psychic mechanism informing it. (Why, I wonder, though, does Žižek put scare quotes around projection, since this is a classic instance of its operation?) He also explains why pleasure should attach to the hyperbolically abject image of the 'Jew' in the films and propaganda of the period. But this should not obscure the limitations of the analysis. It is good on the psychic lining for racism and ethnic prejudice, but does not address the specific ideological, historical and institutional situation in which similar racisms have developed. While anti-Semitism in Germany in the 1930s has an exact historical location in terms of defeat in the First World War, reparations, and the crisis of the economy in the 1920s, in the United States a very different organisation encloses anti-black racism, which has its roots in slavery. And this again is very different from the incredibly violent racism practised by the white South Africans under apartheid, which could not be understood without recognising the kraal mentality and their sense of being overwhelmingly outnumbered in their 'own' country. Or again, English racism, which has always had an imperial meaning going back to the slave plantations (especially for sugar) in the Caribbean in the eighteenth century. It's no accident that in the first modern race riots in London in 1958 Anglo-Caribbean immigrants were set upon by a mob crying 'Black Irish!'

My favourite things

Žižek repeats himself. Almost obsessively, the same ideas and themes recur in his writing. I observe this neutrally – everyone does it. Here are some of his main tropes:

- **Cynical power**. Postmodern power no longer feels a need to conceal itself or its ends. One example is neo-Nazi skinheads who, asked about their violence to foreigners, are happy to rabbit on like social workers, quoting diminished social responsibility, the disintegration of paternal authority, and so on. (I'm not entirely convinced by this.)

- **The structure of the fetish**. The fetishist, according to Freud, typically male, knows his fetish for what it is, but believes in it all the same. In Luis Buñuel's film *That Obscure Object of Desire*, the elderly lover acts as if he does not notice that the woman he loves is really two women, played by two different actresses. He '*knows*' there are really two, but '*acts* as if there is only one' (Žižek 1997: 172). Žižek usually refers psychic fetishism to the Marxist account of commodity fetishism, as he does here.

- **There's always a pay-off**. There is always, despite seemingly obvious disadvantages and absurdities, a pay-off. No mechanism, however apparently negative, can work without a pay-off, which Žižek takes special delight in demystifying. Here the splitting of the two women allows the male subject to project the joint figures of the whore and the faithful maternal wife. (This is classic Freud, exemplied in 'The Universal Tendency towards Debasement in Love', (Freud 1977: 243–60)).

- **Low culture/high theory**. Žižek loves to jump from popular culture to the most serious philosophic arguments. He cites a scene from a Monty Python movie in which two men from 'live organ transplants' demand a woman's liver. When she refuses, they escort her across the universe singing about the billions of stars. How trivial her problems are, in comparison with the galaxies. Žižek compares this to a passage from Kant on the sublime, in which 'the view of a countless multitude of worlds' annihilates 'my importance' (Žižek 1997: 172).

- **The seeming contingency needed for the effect.** Would people be so gripped by Hawking's *A Brief History of Time* if his ruminations about God and the universe did not emanate from 'a crippled, paralysed body' communicating to us through a machine-generated voice (173)?

- **The Obscene Father.** Monty Python again, when John Cleese and his wife are demonstrating to bored schoolboys the penetration of the penis into the vagina and have to shout at one of them to stop looking out of the window: 'enjoyment', comments Žižek, 'is sustained by a superego imperative' (173). This is a Žižek speciality, argued through, for example, in relation to *Totem and Taboo* (see 1991: 24–5). The First Father prevents his son's enjoyment, while keeping all the women for himself. Lacan refers to this as *père-version*, and names the First Father as 'the Great Fucker' (Lacan 1992: 307). Whether it follows that the superego can prohibit obscenity and at the same time make it obligatory is not clear.

- **Multiculturalism v. Universalism.** Multiculturalism does not take seriously the real traumatic kernel of the other, reducing it to folklore. That's about it. Under the pretext of representing the alterity of the other, multiculturalism, a position in any case only available to highly educated Westerners, actually ignores alterity by treating all cultural difference as uniform, not making any distinctions within it.

- **Rape**. There is a conventional argument that, while some women do not want to be raped, there are those who secretly fantasise about it and are therefore complicit with their violator. Žižek makes the point, surely correct, that the most damaging experience would be for a fantasy to be fulfilled in the real (1997: 188). Commenting on a schema from Lacan's *Seminar 20*, Žižek begins by asserting that 'the real' is 'the "hard" traumatic reality which resists symbolisation' (1997: 175). Yet moving on immediately to *jouissance* and the Thing as correlates of the real, he cannot stop himself characterising the real in a particular way. *Jouissance* is 'the abyss of traumatic/excessive enjoyment which threatens to swallow us' (175), down and down like the hero of the Poe story, 'In the Maelstrom'. Isn't there some transference going on here and in similar passages? If we didn't know this was the real, we might well think from the metaphors ('abyss', 'swallow', 'maelstrom') that it was a well-known male fantasy, an implication compounded on the next page when the Thing is compared to 'the stare of Medusa's head' (176).

   There's more to come. In the movie *Angel Heart*, Mickey Rourke and the young woman make love while rain drips into the room. Suddenly the rain turns into blood (a not unfamiliar Hollywood trope, as we see from *The Conversation* and *The Shining* – and *Angel Heart* is in any case a supernaturalist film). Žižek says that the expanding stream of blood announces 'the abyss of lethal jouissance which threatens to engulf us', drawing us 'into a psychotic night in which we are bombarded from all sides by an excessive, unbearable enjoyment' (184). 'Abyss'? 'Engulf'?

   As in the films of David Lynch, 'the disgusting substance of life' is rendered as 'putrefied flesh, crawling with snakes and worms' (66), while one definition of the Lacanian real is that it is the flayed body, the movement of the raw, skinless flesh (1994b: 116). Unveiled, all *jouissance* is the site of a filthy pleasure. But is the 'substance of life' really disgusting? – or is it only disgusting? Surely, like Heidegger's 'es gibt' and Jacques Derrida's 'event' and 'arrival', it must be experienced as both 'positive' and 'negative'?

Coleridge's Ancient Mariner, after killing the albatross, is marooned alone in a total calm and beset by 'slimy things' which crawl 'with legs/Upon the slimy sea'. But later he sees them (though this is not conclusive) as the water snakes, which he blesses as beauteous living things, and the albatross falls from his neck. The 'substance of life' must include putrefying flesh and the flayed body (though Lacan in his early emphasis thought of this as 'the body in pieces'). But life must also comprehend the human embryo, the new-born baby, healthy exercise, cell replacement and our wonderful, million-year-old immune system. Žižek's struggle is to find words for the traumatic kernel of reality, jouissance, the Thing, which he consistently recasts symbolically, while insisting that its status is indeterminable. Žižek's Thing sounds increasingly one-sided and personal.

Examples of Žižek's real

Let me end this list with some examples. In what is now a famous account, the creature in Ridley Scott's *Alien* is said to have the status of 'the pre-symbolic Thing', the 'maternal body', and so 'the living substance of enjoyment' (1989: 79). That there is a maternal association is hard to dispute; like the parasite in Cronenberg's *Shivers*, the alien leaps up into John Hurt's face from an egg-like cell in a huge womb-like structure. When cut with a scalpel, its blood drips onto and through the floors of the spacecraft, slicing through each deck until its force is spent. Žižek says 'the whole reality' is 'utterly defenceless' against it, and that on 'a strongly symbolic level' it 'does not exist' (79).

But wait a minute. Its blood doesn't destroy the ship, and despite its horrifying metamorphoses, Sigourney Weaver is successful in defending herself against it, expelling it into empty space and blasting it by lighting her rocket motors. It *does* exist at a symbolic level, because it is dramatised in a series of signifiers (otherwise we would know nothing about it) and like, perhaps, Duchamp's *Fountain*, it is certainly present at the level of the imaginary, familiar to us from the science fiction films of the 1950s in the trope of the alien from outer space ('It is life, Doctor, but not as we know it'). Ridley Scott does it very well, aided by recently developed technical possibilities.

Kasimir Malevich's painting *The Naked Unframed Icon of my Time* shows a simple black square on a white background. In Žižek's account, reality, the white background, an 'open space' in which objects appear, obtains its consistency only by means of the 'black hole' in its centre. He glosses this as 'the Lacanian *das Ding*, the Thing that gives body to the substance of enjoyment', by changing 'the status of the real into that of a central lack' (1991: 19).

Well, if I were looking for the substance of enjoyment, I would not seek it in this austerely uncompromising yet witty series of paintings by Malevich. Žižek's reading depends on granting priority to the white as space, and on the values he gives to each colour and shape. But in any case, painters have been using the contrast between black and white since the Renaissance as a form of *signification*. And how can we not read Malevich as working precisely to achieve the shock his image produces for a historical culture expecting the frame, especially after Impressionism, to be crowded with the plenitude of light, colour, shape and human variety? This effect can be seen in the kind of minimalism which has become familiar in artists from Malevich to Piet Mondrian and on, notably, to Mark Rothko. The Lacanian Thing? Surely not.

Here is another rather different example (since it comes from the symbolic). During the overthrow of Ceauşescu in Romania, the rebels waved the national flag with the red star, symbol of communism, cut out. Žižek proposes that this meant that in the passage from one 'discourse' to another, a resituating of the syntagmatic chain made 'the hole in the big Other visible' (1993: 1). Leaving aside whether the gaps and the fissures in the Other could ever become properly 'visible', Žižek romanticises the moment as one of pure possibility. But messing about with flags and national symbols has been a time-honoured activity of radical groups (during the Vietnam War Washington saw many versions of the Stars and Stripes). The national flag with the Communist sign excised is surely in the first place an affirmation of traditional Romanian nationalism in a de-Stalinised form? Žižek is a strikingly original and enthusiastic reader of texts, but not always trustworthy, as will be discussed again later.

Finally, in Robert Heinlein's *The Unpleasant Profession of Jonathan Hoag*, the hero tells Randall and Cynthia he has discovered some fundamental flaws in the universe. Later, driving home, Randall asks Cynthia to open the car window. Now, outside, instead of sunshine and a normal city street, all they see is 'a grey and formless mist, pulsing slowly as if with inchoate life' (cited 1991: 14). When Cynthia winds up the window, the normal city is restored. Žižek asks what this mist is, 'if not the Lacanian real, the pulsing of the presymbolic substance in its abhorrent vitality' (14). Perhaps, but there is a similar uncanny effect in Carpenter's *The Fog*. And mist generally is 'grey and formless'. The real causes unbearable anxiety. These are fantasies, and if they were genuinely the real, we could not go near popular culture at all.

Orthodoxy?

Because of Freud's distinction between *Instinkt* and *Trieb*, even the most primitive perceptions are liable to become charged and organised into sets of facilitations. The breast is the breast, but the breast remembered with pleasure is no longer just the breast. In Lacan's terms, the real (of the breast in this case) rapidly becomes a repetition linked to desire. His *Seminar 7* begins from Freud's argument, but goes on to regard *das Ding* as 'the absolute Other of the subject' (Lacan 1992: 52). The Thing is not found, or is found only as something missed. 'One doesn't find it, but only its pleasurable associations' (52). Lacan notes that the relation of mother and child is 'an immense development of the essential character of the maternal thing', that is, of the mother in so far as she occupies the place of *das Ding* (67). What we should particularly remark here, a theme I'll return to, is that there is a connection between the Thing and the speaking subject, structured by a relation of desire, the wish for what appears lost.

Dylan Evans has read Lacan's unpublished seminars, and is sensitive to the way Lacan's concepts change and develop. He is emphatic that 'after the seminar of 1959–60 the term *das Ding* disappears almost entirely from Lacan's work' because it has been reworked as the *objet petit a* from 1963 and the publication of *Seminar 11*. That the Thing in *Seminar 7* is located in the register of the real 'anticipates the transition in Lacan's thought' (1996: 205) which increasingly places the *objet petit a* in the real. Evans believes that 'from the early 1970s', Lacan oscillates between opposing an unknowable 'real' to the 'reality' of psychic representation and reverting to a use of 'real' and 'reality' interchangeably (161).

The real and the symbolic

Orthodoxy aside, there are fundamental reasons why the real should have effects in the other orders. In the middle Lacan of the 1960s, the real is a shy creature, only making rare appearances — in dreams, like the terrible dream Freud refers to when the dead child reproaches the father, saying, 'Father, can't you see I'm burning?' Lacan reads this not as the fulfilment of a wish but as the eruption into fantasy of 'a beyond', 'the real', related perhaps to the father's 'remorse' (1977b: 58–60).

The real is manifest as the symptom, even if the subject misrecognises the fact that it is using its own body to inscribe a meaning it has produced (after 1975 *symptom* is replaced by *sinthome*). And in paranoia, Lacan argues with reference to Schreber, the foreclosure of the Name-of-the-Father leaves a hole in signification, such that the real reappears in the symbolic as hallucination and psychosis (see 1977a: 199–221).

But by far the most fundamental instance of the effect of the real in the symbolic is when a trace or remainder of the subject's Being returns as Meaning, to become the ever-lost cause of desire, the *objet petit a* (Lacan 1977b: 209–13), a point I have pressed already in relation to Judith Butler. Granted that the real does have effects in the symbolic, Lacan wants to safeguard *two* positions. He definitely does not want to be caught subscribing to some version of naturalism or realism by which reality determines subjectivity and culture, in however tenuous a respect (Rorty's comments on Eagleton make the necessity of that very clear). Nor does he want to take the view that the real has no consequences *at all* for culture. So he is adamant that the real appears in signification through a deferral for which the original only occurs in retrospective fantasies: the psychic object is a refound object, its loss a 'consequence of that', refound without our knowing 'except through the refinding, that it was ever lost' (Lacan 1992: 118). I can see that this could be dismissed with a brutal and traditional logic of the either/or. But some of the most crucial work in contemporary thinking – in Heidegger, Adorno, Levinas and Derrida – has concentrated on this necessary impasse. Is Lacan's solution – or are his solutions (since the unconscious is by nature contradictory) – satisfactory? Certainly, the relentless binary logic of an *either* 'in discourse' *or* 'coming from the real' is a much worse solution or, in fact, no solution at all.

If the real affects reality, what can one say about its effects? In broad terms, does the real set limits, as some of Lacan's commentators suggest, encouraged by his acknowledgement in *Seminar 2* of the 'real limitation' that he can't lift the table (1988b: 219)? Žižek's consistent and unequivocal position is that the real produces *excess*. Here he follows the social theories of Laclau and Mouffe, and is backed up to the hilt by Yannis Stavrakakis in *Lacan and the Political* (1999).

Žižek says the real creates excess because it cannot be encountered by the subject, except through idealisation and fantasy. That's right, but the question then would be whether we turn to the real to explain how this excess can give weight to the activity of fantasy (and it should be noted that the gaps in the symbolic order also provoke fantasy). I've made it clear in examples from Žižek that what he writes of as the effects of the real sound on many occasions much more like fantasy, including some fantasies loaded in by Žižek himself.

My example here is one I introduce with trepidation, except that it is mentioned by Žižek himself: the 'symbolic debt' to the dead.

> The two great traumatic events of the holocaust and the gulag are, of course, exemplary cases of return of the dead in the twentieth century. The shadows of their victims will continue to chase us as 'living dead' until we give them a decent burial, until we integrate the trauma of their death into our historical memories.   (1991: 23)

The 'Final Solution' has been the most far-reaching and shattering instance of the real as event in the past half-century. Has this led to idealisation in excess of signification? There are histories, both German and from across the West, films, memoirs, witnesses, testimony, writing of all kinds (some of it, sadly, appropriating the 'Final Solution' for Zionism, see Finkelstein 1997). In a neutral sense, then, an excess. But is any of this large body of work remotely satisfactory? Perhaps only Alain Resnais's half-hour film of 1955, *Nuit et Brouillard*, gets anywhere, and that only because it rests on the premise that this past is irrecoverable, veering at present beyond representation.

In concluding this section, I might risk a speculation. In his earliest writing Lacan gives priority to the imaginary, with essays on the Mirror Stage, for example. In what one might think of as a middle game, when the influence of Saussure and linguistics was strongest, attention fell on the symbolic order (in the *vel* of alienation, for example, Being and Meaning are viewed from a position in the symbolic, since of course a subject actually in Being would be an infant on whom the scar of Meaning and the signifier had not yet been imposed). Development into a last stage would then seem to be an attempt, ordered by mathematical models, to rethink imaginary and symbolic, as it were, from the side of the real.

Žižek as such

'In the last years of Lacan's teaching, however, the accent was shifted from the split between the imaginary and the symbolic to the barrier separating the real from (symbolically structured) reality' (Žižek 1991: vii). This is a clear, manifesto declaration and leaves no doubt where Žižek intends to plant his flag. One might note in passing that in his formulation the imaginary has made a silent exit. Having made some attempt to reconsider issues around earlier and later Lacan, I shall try to assess losses and gains implied, especially for cultural analysis, by Žižek's preference. (Stephen Heath can still serve as model for what you can *do* with the distinction between imaginary and symbolic.)

From imaginary to symbolic

The first price to be paid for disregarding the imaginary and demoting the symbolic is just that: they lose prominence in discussion. My example is Žižek's account of nation and democracy (1991: 162–9). Recalling the 'flare of nationalism' in the Balkans in recent years, Žižek asks where 'the ethnic Cause, the ethnic Thing . . . draws its strength from' (162). He says Lacan sees this strength as 'the reverse of the striving after universality that constitutes the very basis of our capitalist civilisation' (162) (but gives no reference in Lacan for the source of this idea). Because of globalisation, the notions of 'a sovereign nation state, of a national culture' seem 'to lose their weight' (162).

Are they losing their weight? Perhaps it is just that nation states aren't able to eat up smaller states as easily as they did a century ago. Žižek recasts his question by equating the nation with democracy (they are far from identical) and asking, 'who is the subject of democracy?' (163). It is 'the Cartesian subject in all its abstraction', established by every democratic proclamation about '"all the people *without regard to* (race, sex, religion, wealth, social status)"' (163). In this abstraction 'all substantial, innate[!] links' are dissolved, in favour of a 'pure, non-substantial' Cartesian *cogito* (163).

But if the Cartesian *cogito* is indeed non-substantial, does it follow that all subjectivity in which an effect of identity is brought about through identification is also non-substantial? In any case, as Lacan demonstrates in *Seminar 11*, the *cogito* is substantial, structured by an 'I am' in the enounced which depends upon an act of thinking – in words – as its enunciation. All such identity effects are cathected narcissistically, introducing the pleasures of mastery and the promise that you might see yourself seeing yourself. Some of the jubilation of the imaginary in fact.

Democracy, Žižek goes on, is 'fundamentally "anti-humanistic"', not made '"to the measure of (concrete, actual) men" but to the measure of a formal, heartless abstraction', and has no place for the 'fullness of concrete human content, for the genuineness of community links' (163). (It is not clear whether these quotation marks indicate allusions to Lacan. If so, one would like to know where the citations are from.) In any case, this is extraordinary stuff. Surely, these days, whenever such binary oppositions as concrete/abstract, substantial/empty, innate/constructed, humanist/anti-humanist, heartfelt/heartless, genuine/artificial start popping up, alarm bells should sound. Deconstruction of these rather flaky antitheses would begin with the concept of the imaginary, and not only the unconscious charge attached to that (a dangerously volatile charge, as Lacan shows in his essay on aggressivity in *Ecrits* (1977a: 8–29)), but also in the identifications which operate in all forms of collective identity, including the nation-state. Then there are the traditional shared and localised symbolic structures instituted in the discourses, chains of signifiers, meanings, which pervade and 'speak for' those interpellated into a national culture. In *Ecrits* Lacan notes that 'the slightest alteration in the relation between man and the signifier . . . changes the whole course of history by modifying the moorings that anchor his being' (1977a: 174). Nation, I would say, is anchored in a discursive formation, a particular structuring of signification.

Reductive readings

Žižek is more interested in *jouissance*, the Thing and the real than in the signifier. This makes his readings of texts into acts of shocking bravura, rather than something more critically persuasive. It is a bad sign when, talking about *Richard II*, he makes the old quip that 'Shakespeare had read Lacan' (1991: 9). We all have theories, we all give partial interpretations, but some are more partial than others. As previous examples here have already indicated, Žižek is over-anxious to strap his texts to the Procrustean bed of the real.

In Steven Spielberg's well-made film, *Empire of the Sun*, set in Shanghai during the Second World War, the reality of the boy's world, Žižek proposes, is broken when, outside his closeted life, he comes up against the real in the misery and chaos of the Chinese fleeing from the Japanese invaders. His reaction is to hold himself responsible 'for the intrusion of the real'. When that night the Japanese warship enters the harbour, he signals to it from his parents' house with his torch. At exactly this point the ship opens fire. Jim rushes to his father and says, 'I didn't mean it' (Žižek 1991: 29).

Well, yes, and Žižek rightly draws attention to this uncanny moment, but we should not forget what his theoretically correct reading ignores: that it is above all a wild joke, a novel cinematic trope, and a first way to characterise the boy's honesty, his youth, his naivety, his total incomprehension about what's going on, his fantasies of youthful omnipotence (Žižek does refer to his 'phallic gesture of symbolisation', 29), but also, and most importantly for the rest of the movie, the guilt immediately confessed to the father for his arising sexuality.

Žižek links the signalling to a brief sequence later, when Jim massages a dead woman and her eyes fall open for a second, so that Jim is thrown into ecstasy. His feelings of omnipotence are said to be confirmed by 'an answer of the real' (30). Another moment singled out is when Jim is rapt, listening to the last song of the kamikaze pilots at dawn, and joins in as far as he can with a hymn in Chinese. This, says Žižek, reveals 'the object in himself, the *agalma* or hidden treasure that supports his identity' (130). And that's it, very suggestive as far as it goes.

So much is glossed over in this single-minded reading, for example, that the boy's reality is not just any old reality but that of an upper-class English public schoolboy of the 1940s, something that causes him particular problems but, ironically, provides him with a sense of duty and resourcefulness that helps him survive in the camp, especially when he's on his own. Then there is his adolescent sexuality, displaced into an exceptional image when he comes home to his parents' empty house and finds only his mother's scrambled foot-prints in talc spilt on the floor, his ambiguous voyeurism when a couple in the next bed in the camp make love. But more than the loss of the mother, Jim is caught in a protracted struggle to find a father-figure he can identify with: at first the British officers in the camp, though he soon turns from them in disgust at their crass attitudinising towards the Japanese, which only leads them into trouble and mortal danger; he moves from them to the Americans, Basie and the other, but they let him down; so a major theme is his identification with the Japanese and, in a particularly moving way, with the beauty and heroism of the young *kamikaze* pilots, who have acceded completely to castration with such grace and dignity. All this ignores the strikingly phallic aircraft, including the gleaming silver P-51, 'The Cadillac of the Air', and the anti-imperialist, anti-humanist ironies of the text.

My second example can be shorter. In his discussion of *Psycho* (1992: 211–72) Žižek states that the text forces the viewer '*to identify with the abyss beyond identification*' (226). I can't see that anyone would have dared to go to a film that really had that effect, that did not (whatever else) put in its place an intensely felt set of signifiers. Žižek's argument is that the first third of *Psycho* is banal, presided over by the Name-of-the-Father, but after Marion's death the narra-tive moves under the sign of the Desire-of-the-Mother. The mystery of the film lies in 'the rupture' (226) made by 'the intrusion of the Real' in the scene of the murder in the shower, and in the subsequent cut from the drain to Marion's dead eye. We identify with Marion, but Norman Bates 'eludes identification' in so far as he remains 'prisoner of the psychotic drive' and has no access to desire (229–30).

With no main point of identification, surely we'd walk out of the cinema? But of course there is a firm and reasonably attractive point of identification – Norman. Norman, who does desire Marion, and is anxious to protect his mother from public exposure. His mad mother in fact killed Marion (we've heard her savage shouting from the house), and even if we may have doubts, we don't *know* that he is the criminal until the scene at the end, when Marion's sister finds the mummified body in the fruit-cellar. In this respect *Psycho* is like *Oedipus the King*, where we don't know that Oedipus killed his father until the end, or *Hamlet* when certainty that Claudius is a villain is withheld.

Žižek is far too brilliant for this to be a careless or casual misread-ing. A few pages earlier he notes quite happily that when Norman is getting rid of Marion's car in the swamp and it stops sinking for a moment, anxiety 'arises in the viewer – a token of his/her solidarity with Norman' (223). For 'solidarity' read 'identification'? Žižek is not reading for the signifier (though his shot-by-shot analysis of the murder of Arbogast shows he can do it very well); he is not reading for narrative; nor for possibilities of a reader's identification (that is apparently fixed once and for all by the text). Žižek reads for theory and those features which his theory makes visible, and which in turn support the idea of the contrast between reality and the real.

Žižek's fascinating theory of the real often has the consequence of establishing itself as an *object* to which – according to the familiar scenario – there corresponds a subject securely installed (despite denegations) in a metalanguage. For Žižek culture and textuality constitute a knowable totality overseen by a master signifier, the opposition between reality and the real. Difficulties, inexplicable fissures, blank uncertain movements, troubling and obscure textual features are easily washed away with this sponge.

There is, then, always a tension between the persuasiveness of Žižek's reading and our scepticism. For the joyless intellectual — and often for the joyful one – reading Žižek is channel-surfing at a great intellectual height (except that the theory – real/reality – is never too demanding, nor the interpretation too difficult). This tension he tends to negotiate by restlessly moving on, skipping to the next ice floe as each sinks under the weight of our hesitations. There is a high risk of the response, 'You cannot be serious!' And it is no accident – as they used to say in Stalinist circles – that, while widely read, his theoretical and critical tendency has not been much taken up by others.

The subject

The ascription of a central place to the real/reality entails a conceptualisation of the subject. It is not an exaggeration to say that in principle the subject is of no account, for although the whole epic is played out on the terrain of subjectivity, what matters most to Žižek is the real in which the subject vanishes, which overwhelms it, sets it at nothing. There is fantasy and idealisation, but that is not generally where the action is. Further, in so far as the Thing is linked to *jouissance*, sexuality – of a rather special Žižekian character, I would have to say – is given heavy priority almost to the entire exclusion of narcissism, the ego and the imaginary. And identification.

Žižek's manoeuvres around *Psycho* are symptomatic. He says Hitchcock is 'forcing' the viewer to identify with '*the abyss beyond identification*'; meanwhile, he is unconcerned with other possible identifications not catered for in the theory. The case is the same with the cultural events I've already discussed – the *Titanic*, anti-Semitism, nation and, in fact, all the others as well. Žižekian metalanguage has no place for different subjectivities, which for an avowed Lacanian is really rather remarkable.

There is, indeed, as I've suggested myself, an element of shared imaginary and identification, exactly what is set aside in Žižek's analysis of nation. What is missing is a critique of the concept of interpellation. Žižek refers to this frequently, especially in *The Sublime Object*, where he rightly points out that interpellation is never punctual, 'never fully succeeds', though he immediately recoups this excess into his own schema, as 'a stain of traumatic irrationality' (1989: 43). Generally, however, in practice, it suits him to underwrite the Althusserian, functionalist notion of the subject as effect of its interpellation.

Over the last two decades there has been an exciting body of work aimed against the reader as effect of the text and recognising that textuality is always reactivated in and by the reader's desire. This is finely exemplified by Catherine Belsey in *Critical Practice* (1980), setting clear blue water between her account and the pure Althusserian stance. The reader is the effect of the text (of this text not another), but not just an effect of the text, because along with more or less shared positions, he or she will enter different identifications and fantasies afforded by the text and around it. But not in Žižek, for whom the identification is what he says, take it or leave it.

Bypassing the signifier

Have I been unfair in my account of Žižek? But in a sense his own writing is not argued in a way that leaves options besides scepticism or submission. His philosophic work is at the highest level and there is a lot of that. In *Tarrying with the Negative* he criticises the tradition through Kant and Hegel by deploying the enounced/enunciation distinction to show the tangles and attempted resolutions these two giants get into by trying to reconcile object and subject, perception and knowledge, thought and thinking (though Peter Dews is less impressed, see Dews 1995). And in *The Ticklish Subject* there is, I think, a devastating critique of Foucault in four pages (1999: 251–4). A harder, leaner Žižek is emerging as he moves away from cultural and textual analysis (these were my concerns). On that score the conclusion has to be that he is less interested in a study of representations than those moments when, it seems, representation is disrupted. Žižek's preoccupation with the real, an excess, a beyond, an abyss, the unspeakable Thing, rejoins and encourages the line in contemporary critical writing which bypasses the signifier, the mode of address and the complexity of the positions texts make available to subjects.

14 The Two Jakes

It's arguable that between them the two representative figures of Jacques Lacan and Jacques Derrida divide the main possibilities for contemporary thought in the West – with Freud, Kristeva and Zizek on one side, and Foucault, Deleuze and Guattari, Lyotard, Rorty on the other. Yet what interests me is the point of juncture or interface between them. Whenever I read Lacan I think of Derrida, and when I read Derrida I think of Lacan. I don't have a sustained argument leading to a finished conclusion – only a series of 'takes' on places and topics where they touch on each other.

Writing

Both have an intense concern with writing. Lacan, the elder by 29 years, can come first:

> The signifier, producing itself in the field of the Other, makes mani-fest the subject of its signification. But it functions as a signifier only to reduce the subject in question to being no more than a signifier, to petrify the subject in the same movement in which it calls the subject to function, to speak, as subject.   (1977b: 207)

That is from *Seminar 11*, which took place in 1964. In February 1968 Derrida's lecture on 'Differance' included the following:

> *Differance* is not. It is not a being-present, however excellent, unique, principal, or transcendent one makes it. It commands nothing, rules over nothing, and nowhere does it exercise any authority. It is not marked by a capital letter. Not only is there no realm of differance, but differance is even the subversion of every realm. This is what makes it obviously threatening and necessarily dreaded by everything within us that desires a realm, the past or future presence of a realm.   (1973: 153)

Let me propose that the contrast may form a series of (frequently) binary oppositions.

So then: Lacan casual, Derrida careful; Lacan vulgar (he says 'fuck'), Derrida proper (he never would). Lacan's sustained and subordinated syntax has just too many embedded phrases and clauses ever to complete the sense it promises with any security (the 'Lacanian loop'): Derrida, in contrast, paratactic, phrases and clauses qualified in juxtaposition so we can never be sure where the emphasis should come. Lacan irresponsible, Derrida conscientious in the extreme; Lacan speedy Gonzalez, while Derrida is never as slow as he would like (constant interpolations: 'if we had more time . . .', 'if we could take this more slowly . . .'). 'La-can è mobile': Derrida almost uncannily self-consistent, so that one idea from the 1960s contains the germ of the rest discovered retrospectively. To Lacan Derrida concedes (or is it a criticism?) 'the mobility of the discourse' (1987a: 462) – he can hardly hold the same position across one lecture, let alone 20 over one year (*La Chose*, which, as remarked already, figures so hugely in 1960 in *Seminar 7*, has vanished four years later in *Seminar 11*, to be taken up as *objet petit a*).

Lacan the hysteric (as he said himself, he was the complete hysteric for whom *everything* was a symptom): Derrida the obsessive. Lacan defies the father (like Don Juan, always bantering with the Commendatore): Derrida seems the good son who submits to the Father. Lacan, ego and eros: Derrida, the superego. Lacan domination: Derrida imitation. Lacan omnivorously assimilates the world to his teaching (he once said he had nothing except a style): Derrida inhabits the writing of others, unsettling it from within. Lacan against the ego, because his own is so insufferably overweening: Derrida against the ego through denial (if he can't have the full presence he desires then no one can).*

Lacan remarks that it is the strict and punctilious father (like the father of poor Senatspräsident Schreber), who really drives his son mad. Lacan is the comic and indulgent Father, always getting caught

---

* In an interview Derrida explained that during his '"narcissistic" moment of "adolescent" identification', he wanted to be fully autobiographical, desiring '*everything* + n' (1992b: 34–5). He doesn't add that it was the very intensity of his desire for full self-expression which compelled him to recognise the dependence of feeling on words, writing and difference. Lacan never published a book with himself on the cover (though I'm sure he wanted to).

with his pants down (like Noah): Derrida is the Father you could never really please because he would always have a reservation (or two). Lacan's principle: 'I will display the worst about myself so my seduction of you will be the more complete'; Derrida's: 'Take the time to understand me as I deserve and you will never misappropriate me.' Lacan's motto: 'To Hell and back'; Derrida: 'Whatever happens, don't go home'.

Philosophy and psychoanalysis

Can one juxtapose psychoanalysis and philosophy? Lacan is a psychoanalyst (albeit a philosophically informed one) and Derrida a philosopher who works on the margins of philosophy, as well as on the border between literature and philosophy (as in *The Post Card*). Philosophy has no object unless it is other philosophic texts; psychoanalysis claims to provide knowledge of an object, the unconscious, and therefore (especially in the emphasis of Freud) can claim to be another science. Derrida provides a case in point when he cites (*contra* Levinas) Hegel to the effect that vision as a form of sense suspends desire. Hegel follows Kant in the *Third Critique* when he proposes that touch, taste and smell are too gross as forms of perception to be genuinely aesthetic; only sight and hearing are so. Yet Freud in 1905 in the *Three Essays* explains *Schaulust* ('looking pleasure', pompously translated by Strachey as *scopophilia*) as indeed a form of drive both in its voyeuristic and exhibitionist aspects. And he is followed by Lacan, who spends 100 pages of *Seminar 11* analysing Quattrocento representation in terms of conscious and unconscious effects, and so as a functioning of desire. This 'scientific' fact is taken on board by Derrida without demur.

The unhappy affair between Lacan and Derrida

Could Derrida live without Lacan? Both share a view that subjectivity is, 'in words, made of words, others' words', as Beckett says (1958: 139), constituted in language or nowhere. For Lacan the symbolic order, the chains of signifiers, come first; for Derrida there is the inescapable insistence of writing and inscription. For Jacques L. meaning never finally arrives in its place because there is endlessly a 'sliding of the signified under the signifier' (1977a: 160); for Jacques D. meaning always differs and is deferred, so that 'every sign' can be cited, engendering 'infinitely new contexts in an absolutely nonsaturable fashion' (1982: 320). What support, I would have to ask, does the binary opposition between speech and writing gain from the distinction between imaginary and symbolic? What support does the notion of logocentrism take from Lacan's account of the phallus as privileged signifier of difference, and presence from Lacan's *point de capiton*?

Though they only met three times, the relationship between Derrida and Lacan was intense. Around 1970 Lacan seems to have wanted to appropriate the emerging Derrida as the wide-eyed acolyte who would give the philosophic justification to his ideas which Lacan was too busy to fill in (one can imagine how that went down); and in 1971 there are Derrida's remarks to his interviewer in *Positions*, to the effect that his work did abut onto that of the older man, and was perhaps more like his than any other (1987b: 111 n. 3).

One could say that Derrida has made his peace with, come to terms with, every major figure from Plato to Heidegger, but that the signifier of his partial namesake, the other Jake, constantly returns to trouble him, always provoking symptoms of unease, as when, at the start of *Given Time*, Derrida opens his argument that the gift is impossible by referring to Lacan's assertion that love is giving what you don't have – and then appends a page-long footnote making clear that he disapproves entirely of Lacan's implication (1992a: 2–3).

What really drove them apart was an incident so typical of Lacan it could not be invented. In 1991 there was a conference organised by René Major, *Lacan avec les philosophes*, and Derrida made a long concluding statement, 'For the love of Lacan'. Here he explains that after the publication of *Grammatology* in 1967, he received a 'declaration of love' from Lacan, which took the form of a reference in the Introduction to the 1970 edition of the *Ecrits* to 'the instance of the letter before all grammatology' (Derrida 1995b: 711). This must be the context for Derrida's 1975 attack on Lacan in 'Le Facteur de la vérité' ('facteur' means both 'factor' and 'postman').

Where there are no spectres there is no need for exorcism, especially since exorcism always resurrects what it would expel. So it is with the excessive violence unleashed by Derrida's conjuration. How otherwise understand the detail Derrida saves for his last pages, his Parthian shaft, that Lacan (typically, nonchalantly) misquotes (and more than once) the lines from Crébillon's *Atrée* cited in Poe's story, substituting *dessein* ('design') for *destin* ('destiny') (1987a: 495–26). There is no sign from the unforgiving son that the ageing father may have made not a schoolboy howler but a good old-fashioned Freudian slip (for don't we all wish our destiny was a design?).

The text of 'Le Facteur' is now a palimpsest, covered with further writing from Barbara Johnson, Shoshana Felman and others. In Poe's short story *The Purloined Letter*, a detective saves a woman's honour by replacing an incriminating letter she has written with a less incriminating fake. Jake D. levels four charges against Jake L.:

(a) That Lacan's essay is an exercise in 'applied psychoanalysis' (1987a: 425), that it strips away the apparent meaning of Poe's story to reveal the naked truth underneath, a procedure which participates in the great tradition of 'truth-unveiled-woman-castration-shame' (416). Lacan is indicted for using (at least up to 1960) a metalanguage, a 'system of the truth' (462), always expressing himself in 'a writing spiritualised by the voice' (463).

As far as it goes, the accusation is undeniable. But I wonder whether anyone today can escape making some claim to truth if they want to be taken seriously? Surely Jake D. does some unveiling of his own when he strips away Lacan's appearance of telling the truth about Poe's story to show that underneath Lacan can be seen nakedly as an object (and perhaps more than a little feminised?), perpetrating a methodological transcendentalism?

(b) Lacan is committed to a 'phallogocentric transcendentalism' (478) in that his argument assumes the phallus as privileged (Derrida converts this to 'transcendental', 477) signifier of lack, a lack imposed by the men on the erring woman through the form of the letter.

First query: is this phallogocentrism Lacan's, or does it occur in the realm of the unconscious he claims to describe? Should one not recall Juliet Mitchell's assertion in *Psychoanalysis and Feminism* that 'psychoanalysis is not a recommendation *for* a patriarchal society *but* an analysis of one' (1975: xv)? Derrida replies to this form of argument in a footnote to the effect that you are still responsible for the political tendency of your truth (1987a: 481–2).

Second query: Derrida is at great pains to demonstrate that Lacan's conception of the phallus as that which promises to make good the lack it instates is indeed transcendental, so that Lacan's repeated claims that 'no metalanguage can be spoken' and that 'there is no Other of the Other' (1977a: 311) (no guarantee for truth outside the symbolic order itself) are in fact forms of denegation. Derrida knows that for Lacan the phallus is a signifier of lack, but affirms that this lack (represented in the story by the purloined letter itself) 'occupies a determined place with defined contours' (1987a: 425) which renders it immune to dissemination. Lacan's analysis represents a kind of negative theology, therefore.

It can be argued that Derrida treats as a metaphysical concept what is no more than a generalisation from observation.

> The Oedipus complex is so essential to the very dimension of the analytic experience that its pre-eminence is revealed right from the start of Freud's work and is sustained right to its end. This is because the Oedipus complex occupies a privileged position, in the present state of Western civilisation   (Lacan: 1988a: 198)

In Lacan the phallus performs a necessary *function* because it is the signifier which instigates and presides over the transition from Being to Meaning, expelling the infant from apparent self-sufficiency into language and lack. Lacan rereads Freud's castration complex as disrupting the phallic phase, which is the same for girls and boys. What, he asks, is 'the link between the murder of the father and the pact of the primordial law, if it is included in that law that castration should be the punishment for incest?' And he answers his own question by defining the castration complex as the moment that differentiates for the children the man and the woman that they are required to become (1977a: 282). This seems to me some way short of transcendentalism.

(c) Jacques L. argues that Poe's story shows that a letter always reaches its destination; Jacques D., working in terms of writing as difference, flatly denies this: 'a letter does *not always* arrive at its destination'; it never 'truly arrives', there is always 'an internal drifting' (1987a: 489). Here the love affair falls into complete misunderstanding. For Lacan a letter always reaches its destination in the sense outlined in his essay 'The Agency of the Letter', that the letter is the signifier, the only ground of the structure of the unconscious and the symbolic system, which the self-deceptions of the conscious mind would escape and deny, but which always remains there waiting for us.

(d) Why Lacan on Poe, which is so much of a *jeu d'esprit*? Derrida could not – or not so easily – have mounted his attack on almost any other text from Lacan. However, Lacan did place the Poe essay at the head of his edition of the *Ecrits* published in French in 1966. But he excluded it altogether from the English *Ecrits* of 1977. Derrida's letter certainly reached its destination.

(A brief aside: according to *The Postcard*, suddenly and inaccurately in 1979 Lacan revealed to his seminar that Derrida was in analysis, an extravagant, impossible gesture of misappropriation which is absolutely in character. 'Why', Derrida asks, 'does one wish that someone be in analysis?' (1987a: 203).)

The ego and the other

In 'Violence and Metaphysics', on the question of the same and the other, Derrida invokes Parmenides to the effect that '*other than* must be *other than* myself', so that the other 'is no longer absolved of a relation to the ego' (1978: 126). Further down Derrida insists that 'the ego cannot be itself even when it ventures out toward the other', and asks, '*why* is the essential, irreducible, absolutely general and unconditioned form of experience as a venturing forth toward the other still egoity?' (131).

I can see how Lacan might answer Derrida's question: that the big Other, the symbolic order, consists of chains of signifiers linked to each other, which in this respect are indifferent to us; that the ego comes about in the imaginary order when I appropriate myself as myself, an identity borrowed from the mirror, but with the borrowing disavowed; and that the ego is therefore achieved in relation to the symbolic only through fantasy and denial of the order of signifiers on which my identity depends, and which is a precondition for coherent discourse.

In *Logics of Disintegration* Peter Dews comments on the speech/writing opposition that Derrida 'is unable to explain how the experience of meaning is able to occur at all', and offers 'no alternative between the illusory immediacy of speech and the endless delays of writing' (1987: 98–9).

The other (lower case) is always *my* other, a point in the symbolic I imagine as my object, a signifier (or set of signifiers) with which I identify – 'his ego', writes Lacan, 'that is, that which is reflected of his form in his objects' (1977a: 194). Take being in love, for example. In this the relation to the other is irreducibly narcissistic – 'love is essentially deception' – introducing 'a perspective centred on the Ideal point, capital I, placed somewhere in the Other, from which the Other sees me, in the form I like to be seen' (1977b: 268). (This is the gaze of the Other, which sees me from all sides). For Lacan there can be no relation to the other except on the prior basis of the Other, no relation which is not an effect of the order of the signifier, so that any venturing forth toward the other – my other – is fundamentally narcissistic and replete with fantasy and misrecognition.

Derrida's notion of presence relies on Husserl's conception of 'the Living Present', which 'has the irreducible originality of a Now, the ground of a Here' (1989: 136); Husserl's Living Present maintains what Derrida asserts 'must be called the *dialectic* of protention and retention' (58). From Aristotle on we inherit a barely interrogated tradition in which time is imagined as space, that is, a series of identical points along a line, a continuous iteration of the same now: 'Point and time are thought in this circularity which relates them one to the other' (Derrida 1982: 43).

The present 'now' occurs in a relation of difference – from the past now that preceded it (Husserl's retention), from the now anticipated (Husserl's protention). The now, point or *stigme*, depends on another now to define it as past or present, a point which is also the here of a presence in space. 'From Parmenides to Husserl', Derrida concludes,

> the privilege of the present has never been put into question. It could not have been. It is what is self-evident itself, and no thought seems possible outside its element. Nonpresence is always thought in the form of presence.   (1982: 34)

Presence appears to itself in the signified concept, the apparently completed sign. Presence is present as phonocentrism, a supposedly 'absolute proximity of voice and being' which, Derrida asserts, is for Hegel the necessary place of 'the self-presence of the subject' (1976: 12): 'the subject as consciousness has never been able to be evinced otherwise than as self-presence' (1973: 147).

What *is* presence? Presence comes to us from the tradition of logocentrism and, as Derrida acknowledges, it's hard to see how ('at present') we could manage without it, without the 'is', without 'metaphysics'. What is the substance of presence, its conditions of possibility? Derrida suggests that historically it has been an object of desire ('Desire is the desire of presence', 1982: 52); we aim at 'finding again the pleasure or the presence that had been deferred' (1973: 150). Presence is not the same as the 'realm' whose subversion differance instigates, though this argument does imply that the desire for presence is for that narcissistic pleasure which Freud finds we find in the seeming presence of 'His Majesty the Ego'. Presence, then, is lent a psychological substance: 'To think the unique *within* the system, to inscribe it there, such is the gesture of the arche-writing: arche-violence, loss of the proper, of absolute proximity, of self-presence, in truth the loss of what has never taken place, of a self-presence which has never been given but only *dreamed* of [my italics] and always already split, repeated, incapable of appearing to itself except in its own disappearance' (1976: 112). The allusion to 'dream' is not casual: three pages later Derrida refers again to the 'dream of a full and immediate presence' (115).

Derrida's idea of presence has an essentially conceptual realisation. It is like a geometrical point which has position but no extension; or the Marxist conception of ideology as an 'epiphenomenon'; or a subatomic particle realised only for milliseconds in a cyclotron. Or rather, it is an object of desire, existing only as *fantasy*. But what fantasy and how does it work?

For Lacan the imaginary is also an expression of fantasy. It confers identity by maintaining a sense of the individual as substantially located in space and permanent in its temporality. Identity is a provisional but necessary effect achieved by the mechanisms of disavowal and denial which exclude the big Other and the process of the unconscious. Everything not the *I* endangers the *I* flux challenges its permanence, spatial difference its fixity of position, any alterity its identity, any outside its inside. Desire arises beyond the subject and so the subject's desire always overflows and threatens its ego (for Lacan this is the origin of aggression).

Subjectivity

Both Jake L. and Jake D. consider the subject to be an effect of language. For Lacan 'the symbol manifests itself first of all as the murder of the thing, and this death constitutes in the subject the eternalisation of his desire' (1977a: 104); thus the speaking subject appears only to disappear into the defiles of the signifier, language, appropriated by all speaking subjects but belonging to none of them. Being is characterised by 'the particularity' (1977a: 286) of need, that is, the particularity of the infant before he or she enters the universality of the signifier, the shared order of language. Once we do, the subject identifies itself only by losing itself there 'like an object' (1977a: 86).

A not dissimilar drama is played out according to Derrida, but in terms of naming, the possibility and impossibility of a proper name, and 'the play of difference' most signally realised in writing. The proper name 'as the unique appellation reserved for the presence of a unique being' has never *been*, Derrida argues, for it is erased in a system, obliterated from the moment which brings a 'classificatory difference into play' (1976: 109). This is also the moment from which 'there is a "subject"' (108). For Derrida, 'the death of absolutely proper naming, recognising in a language the other as pure other, invoking it as what it is, is the death of the pure idiom reserved for the unique' (110).

Both Jakes insist that any particularity of the subject, whatever might contribute to the presence of a unique being, is cancelled by its necessity to emerge on the universalising, classificatory grounds of language. However, while Derrida begins with a subject *already* foreseen from the side of language, a subject as a proper name, Lacan starts with a 'particularity' which precedes language. This has important consequences.

Any account of the subject as an effect of language faces the problem of how the subject identifies itself within language: Peter Dews asks, 'why the subject should be captured by a specific series of identifications, produce a chain of signifiers which is irreducibly idiosyncratic' (1987: 89). Lacan takes off from the position advanced by Freud when he defines the drive (*Trieb*): 'An instinct [*Trieb*] appears to us as a concept on the frontier between the mental and the somatic, as the psychical representative of the stimuli originating from within the organism and reaching the mind' (1984: 118). Sucking at the breast is an instinctive pleasure we share with the other mammals – but the breast *remembered* (and symbolised so it can be remembered) begins to separate itself from the body and become charged with libido ('oral satisfaction'). Following this cue, Lacan supposes that a pre-linguistic individuality is constituted by the particular materiality of the body as shaped in its earliest days by its place in the family, relationships and the world. The subject is identified by its attempt to refind this bodily self within culture and language.

In illustration Lacan offers a Venn diagram in which Being and Meaning exclude each other. Within the circle of Being the subject is at one with itself but has no meaning; within the Other the subject has meaning but can never be itself. It is, as Lacan says brutally, '*Your money or your life!*' (1977b: 212). Within Meaning the shared area (cross-hatched) represents the unconscious, that is, it is retained as a

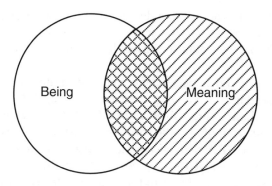

trace around which the subject's identity becomes structured ('If we choose meaning, the meaning survives only deprived of that part of non-meaning that is, strictly speaking, that which constitutes in the realisation of the subject, the unconscious' (211). An example is the heartbreaking case history of Robert in *Seminar 1*. At the level of being Robert is abandoned by his father, and from birth hated, neglected and ill-treated by his mother; not surprisingly, having entered, however partially, the circle of meaning, at the age of three and a half all Robert can say is 'Miss' and 'Wolf' – with the second of which he names everyone – helpers, companions in the orphanage, and, of course, himself (1988a: 91: 100).

However, Derrida can come back against Lacan over subjectivity. Heidegger replaced the category of the subject with *Dasein* and contemptuously dismissed subjectivity as the 'I Thing'. This, however, does not satisfy Derrida, who rejects even Heidegger's radically displaced version of subjectivity, on the grounds that it 'still occupies a place analogous to that of the transcendental subject' (1995a: 273). What Derrida opposes in this interview is the idea of subjects with predicates, the view that subjects are to be defined through an enumeration of 'the essential predicates of which all subjects are the subject'. He continues:

> While these predicates are as numerous and diverse as the type or order of subjects dictates, they are all in fact ordered around being-present [*étant-présent*]: presence to self – which implies therefore a certain interpretation of temporality; identity to self, positionality, property, personality, ego, consciousness, will, intentionality, freedom, humanity, etc.
>
> (1995: 274)

That is: commit yourself to a definition of the subject and you are necessarily committed to an essence, an epistemology, an ontology, and a theory of law; you have closed off the horizon of what it might be to be human.

Does the Lacanian subject have predicates? In the same important interview Derrida concedes that the Lacanian subject does not have 'the traits of the classical subject', but affirms that it remains 'indispensable to the economy of the Lacanian theory' and is also 'a correlate of the law' (256). In Lacan the subject has determinants – determined by the place it is thrown into in the world before it becomes a speaking subject – but across the frontier between body and mind traces of these particular determinants occur within the symbolic order and the circle of meaning as the *objet petit a*. This is the cause of desire, whose substitutes the subject pursues endlessly and impossibly through the defiles of the signifier. Since this subject is present only in its absence, is it a subject with predicates or not?

'La-can è mobile': after 1960 Lacan increasingly stresses how lack, which is, in principle, the cause of the fantasy, appears within the fantasy as its effect (for example, in *Seminar 11* in the rereading of the dream in Freud, 'Father, can't you see I'm burning?'). This gives rise to what I think of as 'the Lacanian loop'. In Freud, 'the finding of an object is in fact a re-finding of it', so that the mother is refound – repeated, with a difference – in the adult sexual object. When Lacan revisits this principle his argument is:

> The object is by nature a refound object. That it was lost is a consequence of that – but after the fact. It is thus refound without our knowing, except through the refinding, that it was ever lost.
>
> (1992: 118)

Lacan's reinscription makes both *finding* and refinding a retrospective effect of the subject's fantasy outside which the object does not exist as a real cause.

Calculation and event

Over the past two decades – and encouraged by Heidegger's contrast between Being There and Being, *es gibt* – Derrida has been reworking his earlier theorisations of difference in the shadow of Levinas and his account of the other, of an ethical imperative which precedes all questions of being and truth, of the absolute obligation to the other, 'the face'. (For Lacan the Other confronts us not with an imperative but an uncertainty, and forces us to ask 'Che vuoi?' – what do you want?). Derrida has reinscribed the other: as (in *Given Time*) the gift, the aporia of the gift ('If you give because you must, then you no longer give' (1992a: 156); as justice on the grounds that justice, if justice is possible, can only be defined as 'gift without exchange' (1992c: 25); as a rethinking of history, another history, without closure, without horizon, in contrast to the closed history predicted by Fukuyama (and fiercely criticised in *Specters of Marx*).

In *The Gift of Death* Derrida reflects on a work by Jan Patočka, *Heretical Essays on the Philosophy of History* (1975) (the line is not clear between what is Patočka and what is Derrida's reading. How could it be?). 'History', states *The Gift of Death*, 'can be neither a decidable object nor a totality capable of being mastered, precisely because it is tied to *responsibility*, to *faith*, and to the *gift*' (1995c: 5). Here Derrida distinguishes between *calculation* and *responsibility*. In its approach to history, calculation consists of 'the technical deployment of a cognitive apparatus, the simple mechanistic deployment of a theorem' (24). With determinate and determinable knowledge there can be no responsibility; responsibility is imposed by what *cannot* be known and foreseen, a form of action or '*decision* that exceeds simple conscience or simple theoretical understanding' (25).

I hope an example of calculation (which I owe to Rob Lapsley) is not too naïvely empiricist to make a more general point. In 1917 Lenin and the other leaders, having achieved a crucial position in Russian politics which demonstrated that they were pretty shrewd in calculation, discussed whether to go for a full-scale uprising. Lenin's view, which won the day, was that Russia was the 'weakest link' in the capitalist chain and that, although it had not in any proper Marxist sense achieved the historical development at which such an event became possible, nevertheless if they went for it now, a Revolution in Russia would be a signal to the rest of the proletariat of Europe, who would immediately rise in support (in France, Britain, Germany and elsewhere), thus – retrospectively – conferring mature success on the Russian intervention. Lenin certainly engaged in 'the technical deployment of a cognitive apparatus'; the Bolsheviks did come to power in Russia; but Lenin's wider calculation couldn't have been more wrong. My query is: how can calculation, as something subjects do, ever happen untrammelled by fantasy and misrecognition?

Similar doubts occur against Derrida's idea of responsibility and event. Unforeseen events are not always bad – in an interview of 1994 Derrida says:

> The kind of absolute arrivals I am trying to describe are similar to births, the arrival of babies. . . . The family anticipates . . . it prepares the way. . . . But despite all the anticipations . . . the element of chance cannot be eliminated: the child that arrives is always unforeseen. It speaks of itself from the *origin* of a different world, or from a *different* origin of this one.   (1994b: 32)

However, with the event, the issue of subjectivity returns with perhaps greater pertinence. In *Politics of Friendship* Derrida is explicit about an incommensurability between subjectivity and event:

> Certainly the decision makes the event, but it also neutralizes this happening that must surprise both the freedom and the will of every subject – surprise, in a word, the very subjectivity of the subject, affecting it wherever the subject is exposed, sensitive, receptive, vulnerable and fundamentally passive, before and beyond any decision – indeed, before any subjectivation or objectivation. Undoubtedly the subjectivity of a subject, already, never decides anything; its identity in itself and its calculable permanence make every decision an accident which leaves the subject unchanged and indifferent. *A theory of the subject is incapable of accounting for the slightest decision.*   (1997: 68)

This follows Freud to the letter: subjectivity is developed (develops itself) precisely as a psychic system to which nothing can happen, no event be wholly unforeseen. Through the mechanism of deferral (*Nachträglichkeit*) it reinterprets the new as the already experienced, while the simultaneous existence of the systems *perception/consciousness* and the *unconscious* has evolved to reduce the intensity of external stimulations to what is manageable by the apparatus. At the end of 'The Mystic Writing Pad' Freud writes: 'It is as though the unconscious stretches out feelers, through the medium of the system *Pcpt.-Cs.*, towards the external world and hastily withdraws them as soon as they have sampled the excitations coming from it' (1984: 434). If the stimuli are simply too shattering for the system to cope with (in Freud's example, the trenches of the First World War caused some soldiers to go into 'shell-shock'), the system overloads, as it were, cannot process the incoming, compulsively repeats it. In Lacan's phrasing the effect is no different: even a penetrating *image* of the real, 'of the real lacking any possible mediation, of the ultimate real, of the essential object which isn't an object any longer', something 'faced with which all words cease and all categories fail', this is 'the object of anxiety *par excellence*' (1988b: 164). My question would be: could anyone experience a Derridean 'event' – absolutely beyond calculation, anticipation or fantasy – without the risk of *trauma*?

Transparency and misrecognition

In 'Violence and Metaphysics' Derrida recalled how Levinas argues that Heidegger remains a philosopher of light – and so power – discriminating between inside and outside, giving life to the opposition of subject and object. Heidegger does this because he relies on a contrast between the 'false consciousness' of the *Mitsein* and 'the collectivity of the with', *Miteinandersein*, whose 'authentic form is revealed around the truth' (1978: 90). Reading the two Jakes alongside each other, a similar question may arise about transparency of access – to calculation (defined apparently beyond the possibility of self-deception), the event (given apparently in terms impossible for subjectivity) and the other (which imposes an absolute obligation which can be defined but not, it seems, misrecognised).

These anxieties overlap with the criticism put forward by Ernesto Laclau of Derrida's later, ethical stance on alterity:

> . . . from the fact that there is the impossibility of ultimate closure and presence, it does not follow that there is an ethical imperative to 'cultivate' the openness or even less to be necessarily committed to a democratic society. I think that the latter can certainly be defended from a deconstructionist perspective, but that defense cannot be logically derived from constitutive openness – something more has to be added to the argument. Precisely because of the undecidability inherent in constitutive openness, ethico-political moves different from or even opposite to a democracy 'to come' can be made. . . . In that way a case for totalitarianism can be presented starting from deconstructionist premises.   (Laclau 1995: 93)

How does the other compel us to respond as Derrida supposes? Can subjectivity – whose very possibility Derrida works so hard to eliminate – ever be excluded from the encounter with alterity? In *The Gift of Death* Derrida asserts that absolute responsibility means I must always make the sacrifice of Abraham, but I confront the aporia that in fulfilling one responsibility, I give up 'my obligations to the other others whom I know or don't know, the billions of my fellows (without mentioning the animals . . .)' (1995c: 69).

Kierkegaard discriminates between the 'aesthetic', 'the ethical' and the 'spiritual' lie, taking up the Biblical account of Abraham's sacrifice of Isaac (Genesis 22: 1–19) as a paradigm of the absolute obligation to be answered in the spiritual life. Derrida draws on the example for his own purposes, to argue that in not helping everyone in need we are unlike Abraham, willing even to sacrifice the only son of his old age.

In *Mimesis*, Erich Auerbach gives a rhetorical reading of the Genesis narrative against the Homeric story of the housekeepers recognising the scar of Odysseus on his return home at last. Auerbach's contrast makes an unsurpassed rhetorical analysis of the two originating stories in the two traditions, in the form of binary oppositions (1953: 3–23):

HOMER / GENESIS
- externalised, uniformly focused phenomena / externalisation only of phenomena necessary for narrative;
- definite time and place / time left undefined, obscure;
- perpetual foreground, no lacunae / background indicated;
- thoughts and feeling expressed / thoughts, feeling unexpressed;
- leisurely narrative, little suspense / unrelieved suspense directed at single goal;
- pure present / no present, a blank duration;
- legend / legend, though the Elohist 'had to believe in the objective truth of the story'.

Aware that you could characterise Hellenic/Judaic by a series of oppositions like this, modern writers such as Nietzsche and Ezra Pound have taken it as their aim to expel Judaism from Western culture – an impossible project, since Judaism is inseparable from Christianity (the Middle Ages gave the story of Abraham its own typological rereading – Abraham as God and Isaac as Jesus, for example, including the happy ending). Derrida has deliberately aimed to deconstruct the opposition into 'Jewgreek is greekjew' (1978: 153), as Joyce says in *Ulysses*.

The part which concerns me most is this:

> And it came to pass after these things, that God did tempt Abraham, and said unto him, Abraham: and he said, Behold, here I am. And he

said, Take now thy son, thine only son Isaac, whom thou lovest, and
get thee into the land of Moriah; and offer him there for a burnt offering upon one of the mountains which I will tell thee of.

(Genesis 22: 1–2)

And Abraham does it. Auerbach asks, 'Where are the two speakers?
We are not told. . . . God, in order to speak to Abraham, must come
from somewhere, and enter the earthly realm from some unknown
heights or depths. Whence does He come, when does He call to
Abraham? We are not told' (1953: 8). As for Abraham, 'where is he? We
do not know'. As Auerbach points out, the Hebrew translated as 'here
I am', Hinne-Ni, means 'only something like "behold me"', with no
specification of place (8).

If there is no speech, there are no speakers and, as Auerbach
suggests, it is hard for speakers not to be situated somewhere. From
the beginning, Derrida's project has been to demonstrate the impossibility of logocentrism and direct access to thought outside signification. In his two books on Husserl he makes a cogent and, I say,
unassailable case against belief that there can be any form of inner
speech, or inner consciousness, or silent intuition which does not
depend on signification. It's quite a change that 'God said' gets such
an easy passage. And if there is language – speech or writing –
between two subjects, where language is misconceived as transparent, as though meaning could pass through it as through a clear pane
of glass, there is dissemination, recontextualisation and the necessity
of interpretation. Consider Hamlet. His father's Ghost speaks to him
when they are alone and lays this injunction upon him:

GHOST: If thou didst ever thy dear Father love –
HAMLET: Oh God!
GHOST: Revenge his foul and most unnatural murder.

(*Hamlet*, I.iv.5)

(As far as I can see, this exchange is not referred to in *Specters of
Marx*, 1994a.) If Laertes had been placed in this situation, Claudius
would only have had ten minutes to live. The command seems fairly
unequivocal, but Hamlet, more modern than Laertes, has trouble, as
the rest of the action shows, with every term, particularly, 'revenge'
and 'murder', not to mention the conditional form of the order 'if
thou didst ever' (for what son could ever say he loved, and ever loved,
his father?). I wonder if the voice of God or old Hamlet speaks in the

tones of the Other, or rather, in those more like the superego – impossible, unconditional, irreconcilable, exorbitant?

At conferences I have sometimes listened to earnest young Derrideans intone with the utmost seriousness our absolute obligation to the Other. I am not so confident what the Other would be if it ever addressed me.

Consider. If God stands on my doorstep and says I have to sacrifice my son (and I do have a son), what my responses would be (and yours?):

'Sorry, not here, try next door.'

And if God returned:

'You cannot be serious.'

'Show me your badge, licence, authorisation.'

'I wasn't expecting the Spanish Inquisition.'

'Who are you to tempt me with my own desires?'

Lacan's position is that speaking subjects are separated from each other by 'the wall of language' (Lacan, 1988a: 244). What the Other, the big Other, of the symbolic order, excites in us – all it can do for us – does not come in any form of duty or imperative. Rather, it leads to uncertainty, to the 'Che vuoi?', the radical question, 'What do you want?'. But we cannot know what the Other wants of us because it constitutes our own desire.

If he were still with us, Lacan would have taken a specially sardonic pleasure in exposing the touch of Schreber here in this paranoiac fantasy of a world where I might be responsible for *everything* (including the animals). Can we ever repeat too much Lacan's warning against 'the mirage that renders modern man so sure of being himself even in his uncertainties about himself, and even in the mistrust he has learned to practise against the traps of self-love' (1977a: 165)?

15   Conclusion

There is without doubt some justice in the counter-arguments. Lacan has been accused of undue systematicity and a nostalgia for the truth of full speech. Stephen Heath might have difficulty in integrating the unconscious fully into his account of ideology's production of an imaginary position for the subject. But this need not be the end of the story.

My thesis – which I am not too shy to state – is that for any text there is always an imaginary, one never entirely the same as the text may claim for itself, but one that is not entirely different either (or so different, at least, that it can entirely disregard the one the text is sure of claiming for itself). That imaginary, its conditions, its implications, its overall aims, has a political impact.

Of course, any text can be, is, and ought to be read against the grain. It would be perfectly possible to read even this little text for what it says without meaning to (that lies in the nature of the imaginary). You could, if you wanted to, collate the unguarded metaphors (especially with an eye, say, to inside/outside, parasite/host, centre/margin and the rest in the not unfamiliar litany). You could (I'd be tempted to do it myself if it were less boring) look at a certain overuse of irony that is almost inescapable for an English writer to show how it evades, exceeds, unsettles the very thing it is trying to say; you could single out parts where the text in its own denegations relies on a sense of totality it officially disowns. And so on.

But wouldn't that be a rather empty exercise? And wouldn't it unwittingly confirm a main contention put forward here – that the privileging of difference presumes an imaginary wholeness before it can set to its task of celebrating difference?

Not much of a conclusion, but still I'll try to spell it out. You need to move beyond the traditional humanism of the subject – the centrality of agency, the primacy accorded to a supposedly un-self-deceived consciousness, the transcendental ego. My argument has been that you cannot on that count do without the ego, the imaginary, *altogether*. But if you do move past humanism, there seem to be two options. Either horizons have no limit, the subject subsists not even as any kind of position, but merely as endless transformation. Or there is a subject and it is in the last instance closed. However, the last instance is deflected asymptotically by a desire (so the lonely hour of closure never comes) predetermined ultimately, if not immediately, as Darwinian and species–species.

An aporia compelling us into practice? Or an impasse we cannot think past?

References

Ahmad, Aijaz (1992) *In Theory: Classes, Nations, Literatures* (London: Verso).

Althusser, Louis (1969) *For Marx*, trans. Ben Brewster (Harmondsworth: Penguin).

—— (1977) *Lenin and Philosophy*, trans. Ben Brewster (London: New Left Books).

Auerbach, Erich (1953) *Mimesis: The Representation of Reality in Western Literature*, trans. Willard R. Trask (Princeton, NJ: Princeton University Press).

Barthes, Roland (1972) *Mythologies*, trans. Annette Lavers (London: Jonathan Cape).

—— (1977) *Image–Music–Text*, trans. Stephen Heath (London: Fontana).

Beckett, Samuel (1958) *The Unnameable* (New York: Grove Press).

Belsey, Catherine (1980) *Critical Practice* (London: Methuen).

Benveniste, Emile (1971) *Problems in General Linguistics*, trans. Mary Elizabeth Meek (Coral Gables, FL: University of Miami Press).

Bhabha, Homi K. (1983) 'Difference, Discrimination, and the Discourse of Colonialism', *The Politics of Theory*, ed. Francis Barker, Margaret Iverson and Diana Loxley (Colchester: University of Essex) pp. 194–211.

—— (1994) *The Location of Culture* (London: Routledge).

Botting, Fred (1999) *Sex, Machines and Navels: Fiction, Fantasy and History in the Future Present* (Manchester: Manchester University Press).

Braidotti, Rosi (1994) *Nomadic Subjects: Embodiment and Sexual Difference in Contemporary Feminist Theory* (New York: Columbia University Press).

Bryson, Norman (1983) *Vision and Painting: The Logic of the Gaze* (London: Macmillan – now Palgrave).

Butler, Judith (1990) *Gender Trouble: Feminism and the Subversion of Identity* (New York: Routledge).

—— (1993) *Bodies that Matter: On the Discursive Limits of 'Sex'* (New York: Routledge).

Copjec, Joan (1994) 'Sex and the Euthanasia of Reason', *Supposing the Subject*, ed. Joan Copjec (London: Verso) pp. 16–44.

Derrida, Jacques (1973) 'Differance', *'Speech and Phenomena' and Other Essays on Husserl's Theory of Signs*, trans. David B. Allison (Evanston, IL:

Northwestern University Press) pp. 129–60.

—— (1976) *Of Grammatology*, trans. Gayatri Spivak (Baltimore, MD: Johns Hopkins University Press).

—— (1978) *Writing and Difference*, trans. Alan Bass (London: Routledge).

—— (1982) *Margins of Philosophy*, trans. Alan Bass (London: Harvester).

—— (1987a) *The Post Card: From Socrates to Freud and Beyond*, trans. Alan Bass (Chicago, IL: University of Chicago Press).

—— (1987b) *Positions*, trans. Alan Bass (London: Athlone).

—— (1989) *Edmund Husserl's 'Origin of Geometry'*, trans. John. P. Leavey (Lincoln, NE: University of Nebraska Press).

—— (1991) *A Derrida Reader: Between the Blinds*, ed. Peggy Kamuf (Hemel Hempstead: Harvester Wheatsheaf).

—— (1992a) *Given Time: 1. Counterfeit Money*, trans. Peggy Kamuf (Chicago, IL: University of Chicago Press).

—— (1992b) *Acts of Literature*, ed. Derek Attridge (New York: Routledge).

—— (1992c) 'Force of Law: The "Mystical Foundation of Authority"', *Deconstruction and the Possibility of Justice*, ed. Drucilla Cornell, Michel Rosenfeld and David Gray Carlson (New York: Routledge).

—— (1994a) *Specters of Marx: The State of the Debt, the Work of Mourning and the New International*, trans. Peggy Kamuf (New York: Routledge).

—— (1994b) 'The Deconstruction of Actuality: An Interview with Jacques Derrida', trans. Jonathan Rée, *Radical Philosophy* 68, 28–41.

—— (1995a) *Points . . . : Interviews, 1974–1994*, ed. Elisabeth Weber (Stanford, CA: Stanford University Press).

—— (1995b) 'For the Love of Lacan', trans. Brent Edwards and Ann Lecercle, *Cardozo Law Review* 16, 699–728.

—— (1995c) *The Gift of Death*, trans. David Wills (Chicago, IL: University of Chicago Press).

—— (1997) *Politics of Friendship*, trans. George Collins (London: Verso).

Dews, Peter (1987) *Logics of Disintegration* (London: Verso).

—— (1995) 'The Tremor of Reflection: Slavoj Žižek's Lacanian Dialectics', *Radical Philosophy* 72, 17–29.

Dollimore, Jonathan (1991) *Sexual Dissidence: Augustine to Wilde, Freud to Foucault* (Oxford: Clarendon Press).

Donnelly, James S., Jr (1993) 'The Great Famine: Its Interpreters, Old and New', *History Ireland* 1, no. 3, 27–33.

Eagleton, Terry (1991) *Ideology: An Introduction* (London: Verso).

—— (1995) *Heathcliff and the Great Hunger: Studies in Irish Culture* (London: Verso).

Easthope, Antony (1983) *Poetry as Discourse* (London: Methuen).

—— (1989) *Poetry and Phantasy* (Cambridge: Cambridge University Press).

—— (1999) *Englishness and National Culture* (London: Routledge).

Eco, Umberto (1979) *The Role of the Reader: Explorations in the Semiotics of Texts* (Bloomington, IN: Indiana University Press).

Edmond, Rod (1995) 'Much Ado About Difference', *Radical Philosophy* 72, 38–40.

Eliot, T. S. (1936) *Collected Poems 1909–35* (London: Faber).

—— (1951) *Selected Essays* (London: Faber).

Ellis, John (ed.) (1977) *Screen Reader 1: Cinema/Ideology/Politics* (London: Society for Education in Film and Television).

Elster, Jon (1985) *Making Sense of Marx: Studies in Marxism and Social Theory* (Cambridge: Cambridge University Press).

Evans, Dylan (1996) *An Introductory Dictionary of Lacanian Psychoanalysis* (London: Routledge).

Feyerabend, Paul (1981) *Problems of Empiricism. Philosophical Papers*, vol. 2 (Cambridge: Cambridge University Press).

Finkelstein, Norman (1997) 'Daniel Jacob Goldhagen's "Crazy" Thesis: A Critique of *Hitler's Willing Executioners*', *New Left Review*, 224 (July–August), 39–88.

Foucault, Michel (1979) *The History of Sexuality*, vol. 1: *An Introduction*, trans. Robert Hurley (London: Allen Lane).

—— (1980) *Power/Knowledge: Selected Interviews and Other Writings, 1972–77*, ed. Colin Gordon (Brighton: Harvester).

—— (1982) 'Afterword: The Subject and Power', *Michel Foucault: Beyond Structuralism and Hermeneutics*, ed. Herbert L. Dreyfus and Paul Rabinow (Brighton: Harvester) pp. 208–26.

Freud, Sigmund (1976) *The Interpretation of Dreams*, ed. Angela Richards, Penguin Freud Library 4 (Harmondsworth: Penguin).

—— (1977) *On Sexuality*, ed. Angela Richards, Penguin Freud Library 7 (Harmondsworth: Penguin).

—— (1979) *On Psychopathology*, ed. Angela Richards, Penguin Freud Library 10 (Harmondsworth: Penguin).

—— (1984) *On Metapsychology: The Theory of Psychoanalysis*, ed. Angela Richards, Penguin Freud Library 11 (Harmondsworth: Penguin).

Fuchs, R. H. (1980) *Richard Long* (New York: The Solomon R. Guggenheim Foundation).

Grossberg, Lawrence, Cary Nelson and Paula Treichler (eds) (1992) *Cultural Studies* (New York: Routledge).

Hackett, Francis (1919) *Ireland: A Study in Nationalism* (New York: B. W. Huebsch).

Haraway, Donna J. (1991) *Simians, Cyborgs, and Women: The Reinvention of Nature* (London: Free Association Books).

Heath, Stephen (1976) '*Jaws*, Ideology and Film Theory', *Times Higher Education Supplement*, 26 March, p. 11.

—— (1976–7) '*Anata mo*', *Screen* 17: 4, 49–66.

—— (1981) *Questions of Cinema* (London: Macmillan – now Palgrave).

Heidegger, Martin (1962) *Being and Time*, trans. John Macquarrie and Edward Robinson (Oxford: Blackwell).

Hindess, Barry and Paul Hirst (1977) *Mode of Production and Social Formation* (London: Macmillan – now Palgrave).

Hirst, Paul (1979) *On Law and Ideology* (London: Macmillan – now Palgrave).

Hoggart, Richard (1958) *The Uses of Literacy* (Harmondsworth: Penguin).

Hull, Carrie L. (1997) 'The Need in Thinking: Materiality in Theodor Adorno and Judith Butler', *Radical Philosophy* 84, 22–35.

Hutchinson, John and Anthony D. Smith (eds) (1996) *Ethnicity* (Oxford: Oxford University Press).

Jakobson, Roman (1960) 'Closing Statement: Linguistics and Poetics', *Style in Language*, ed. Thomas Sebeok (Cambridge, MA: MIT Press) pp. 350–77.

—— (1971) 'Shifters, Verbal Categories, and the Russian Verb', *Selected Writings*, vol. II: *Word and Language* (The Hague: Mouton) pp. 130–47.

Judovitz, Dalia (1995) *Unpacking Duchamp: Art in Transit* (Berkeley, CA: University of California Press).

Kristeva, Julia (1984) *Revolution in Poetic Language*, trans. Margaret Waller (New York: Columbia University Press).

—— (1992) 'The System and the Speaking Subject' (1973), repr. in Antony Easthope and Kate McGowan (eds), *A Critical and Cultural Theory Reader* (Open University Press: Buckingham) pp. 77–80.

Kuhn, Thomas S. (1970) *The Structure of Scientific Revolutions* (Chicago, IL: University of Chicago Press).

Lacan, Jacques (1972) 'Of Structure as an Inmixing of an Otherness Prerequisite to Any Subject Whatever', *The Structuralist Controversy*, ed. Richard Macksey and Eugenio Donato (Baltimore, MD: Johns Hopkins University Press) pp. 186–200.

—— (1977a) *Ecrits: A Selection*, trans. Alan Sheridan (London: Tavistock).

—— (1977b) *The Four Fundamental Concepts of Psychoanalysis* (*Seminar 11*), trans. Alan Sheridan (Harmondsworth: Penguin).

—— (1977c) 'Desire and Interpretation of Desire in *Hamlet*', trans. James Hulbert, *Yale French Studies*, 55/56 (1977), 11–52.

—— (1988a) *The Seminar of Jacques Lacan: Book I*, trans. John Forrester (Cambridge: Cambridge University Press).

—— (1988b) *The Seminar of Jacques Lacan: Book II*, trans. Sylvana Tomaselli (Cambridge: Cambridge University Press).

—— (1992) *The Ethics of Psychoanalysis, 1959–60* (*Seminar 7*), trans. Dennis Porter (London: Tavistock/ Routledge).

—— (1998) *On Feminine Sexuality: The Limits of Love and Knowledge* (*Encore*) (*Seminar 20*), trans. Bruce Fink (New York: Norton).

Laclau, Ernesto (1995) ' "The Time is Out of Joint" ', *Diacritics* 25, no. 2, 86–96.

Laclau, Ernesto and Chantal Mouffe (1985) *Hegemony and Socialist Strategy: Towards a Radical Democratic Politics*, trans. Winston Moore and Paul Cammack (London: Verso).

Laplanche, Jean and Jean-Bertrand Pontalis (1973) *The Language of Psychoanalysis*, trans. Donald Nicholson-Smith (New York: Norton).

Lapsley, Robert and Michael Westlake (1988) *Film Theory: An Introduction* (Manchester: Manchester University Press).

Lapsley, Rob and Michael Westlake (1993) 'From *Casablanca* to *Pretty Woman*: The Politics of Romance', in *Contemporary Film Theory*, ed. Antony Easthope (London: Longman) pp. 179–203.

Latham, Rob (1992) 'Cultural Studies and Science Fiction', *Science Fiction Research Association Review*, 198 (June).

Loomba, Ania (1998) *Colonialism/Postcolonialism* (London: Routledge).

Lyotard, Jean-François (1984) *The Postmodern Condition: A Report on Knowledge*, trans. Geoff Bennington and Brian Massumi (Manchester: Manchester University Press).

—— (1989) *The Lyotard Reader*, ed. Andrew Benjamin (Oxford: Blackwell).

Marsden, Jill (1996) 'Virtual Sexes and Feminist Futures: The Philosophy of Cyberfeminism', *Radical Philosophy* 78, 6–18.

Marx, Karl (1973) *Grundrisse*, trans Martin Nicolaus (Harmondsworth: Penguin).

—— (1977) *Selected Writings*, ed. David McLellan (Oxford: Oxford University Press).

Marx, Karl and Frederick Engels (1950) *Selected Works*, 2 vols (London: Lawrence and Wishart).

Merleau-Ponty, Maurice (1965) *The Structure of Behaviour*, trans. Alden L. Fisher (London: Methuen).

Miller, David (1995) *On Nationality* (Oxford: Clarendon Press).

Milton, John (1968) *Poems*, ed. John Carey and Alastair Fowler (London: Longman).

Mitchell, Juliet (1975) *Psychoanalysis and Feminism* (Harmondsworth: Penguin).

Mitchell, Juliet and Jacqueline Rose (1985) *Feminine Sexuality: Jacques Lacan and the Ecole Freudienne* (New York: Norton).

Moi, Toril (1985) *Sexual/Textual Politics* (London: Methuen).

Mulvey, Laura (1992) From 'Visual Pleasure and Narrative Cinema', repr. in Antony Easthope and Kate McGowan (eds), *A Critical and Cultural Theory Reader* (Buckingham: Open University Press) pp. 158–66.

Parry, Benita (1994) 'Signs of Our Times: A Discussion of Homi Bhabha's *The Location of Culture*', *Third Text* 28/9, 5–24.

Plath, Sylvia (1981) *Collected Poems,* ed. Ted Hughes (London: Faber).

Pound, Ezra (1954) *Literary Essays,* ed. T. S. Eliot (London: Faber).

—— (1960) *Gaudier-Brzeska: A Memoir* (Hessle, Yorks.: Marvell Press).

Quinton, Anthony (1980) *Francis Bacon* (Oxford: Oxford University Press).

Richter, Hans (1965) *Dada: Art and Anti-Art,* trans. David Britt (London: Thames and Hudson).

Rorty, Richard (1980) *Philosophy and the Mirror of Nature* (Oxford: Blackwell).

Rose, Jacqueline (1991) *The Haunting of Sylvia Plath* (London: Virago).

Said, Edward (1993) *Culture and Imperialism* (London: Chatto and Windus).

—— (1995) *Orientalism* (Harmondsworth: Penguin).

—— (1999) 'On Writing a Memoir', *London Review of Books,* 29 April.

Sandford, Stella (1999) 'Contingent Ontologies: Sex, Gender and "Woman" in Simone de Beauvoir and Judith Butler', *Radical Philosophy* 97, 18–28.

Saussure, Ferdinand de (1992) From *Course in General Linguistics,* repr. in Antony Easthope and Kate McGowan (eds), *A Critical and Cultural Theory Reader* (Buckingham: Open University Press) pp. 7–13.

Shakespeare, William (1982) *Hamlet,* ed. Harold Jenkins (London: Methuen).

Sinfield, Alan (1998) *Gay and After* (London: Serpent's Tail).

Stavrakakis, Yannis (1999) *Lacan and the Political* (London and New York: Routledge).

Tzara, Tristan (1992) From 'Memoirs of Dadaism', repr. in Antony Easthope and Kate McGowan (eds), *A Critical and Cultural Theory Reader* (Buckingham: Open University Press) pp. 233–6.

Wittgenstein, Ludwig (1967) *Philosophical Investigations,* trans. G. E. M. Anscombe (Oxford: Blackwell).

Woodham-Smith, Cecil (1962) *The Great Hunger: Ireland, 1845–9* (London: Hamish Hamilton).

Yeats, W. B. (1958) *Collected Poems* (London: Macmillan – now Palgrave).

Young, Robert (1990) *White Mythologies: Writing History and the West* (London: Routledge).

—— (1995) *Colonial Desire: Hybridity in Theory, Culture and Race* (New York: Routledge).

Žižek, Slavoj (1989) *The Sublime Object of Ideology* (London: Verso).

—— (1991) *Looking Awry: An Introduction to Jacques Lacan Through Popular Culture* (Cambridge, MA: MIT Press).

—— (1992) *Everything You Always Wanted to Know about Lacan (But Were Afraid to Ask Hitchcock)* (London: Verso).

—— (1993) *Tarrying with the Negative: Kant, Hegel and the Critique of Ideology* (Durham, NC: Duke University Press).

—— (1994a) 'Introduction: The Spectre of Ideology', *Mapping Ideology*, ed. Slavoj Žižek (London: Verso) pp. 1–33.

—— (1994b) *Metasteses of Enjoyment* (London: Verso).

—— (1997) *The Plague of Fantasies* (London: Verso).

—— (1999) *The Ticklish Subject: The Absent Centre of Political Ontology* (London: Verso).

Index

University of Glamorgan
Prifysgol Morgannwg
Learning Resources
Centre